Molly's Memoir
by

Deanna Edens

Text copyright © 2015 Deanna Edens
All rights reserved.

Cover Photograph by Tomert@DepositPhotos

Acknowledgements
Special thanks to Cheryl Estrada, Nancy Holloway, Barbara L. Jones, Pam Tindell, Geneva Lacy, David Robert Edens Jr., and Ella Bokey for providing editing advice.

Some of the anecdotal illustrations in this book are true to life and are included with the permission of the persons involved. All other illustrations are composites of real situations, and any resemblance to people living or dead is entirely coincidental.

This story is a work of fiction.

Proceeds earned from this book are donated to the Monroe County Humane Society.

Other Books by Deanna Edens

The Convenience of Crafting Maple Fudge
Welcome to Bluewater Bay
Christmas Comes to Bluewater Bay
Mystery in Bluewater Bay
Love Blooms in Bluewater Bay
The Adventures of the Bluewater Bay Sequinettes:
The complete Bluewater Bay Series
Angels of the Appalachians
Erma's Attic

"Nothing is so common as the wish to be remarkable."
William Shakespeare

Forward

While working part-time at the Springfield Senior Care Facility, I was drafted by two gray-haired, knee-high wearing women in their eighties to inscribe the instances contained within this memoir. At the time, I was attending college and majoring in journalism, but since this delightful occasion, my interest switched from documenting current events to composing biographies for folks from all over the world. I found that times gone by – the sorrows, joys, accomplishments, and disappointments that make up an amazing life – are much more thought provoking than the discouraging current events overwhelming our world today.

By the time this biography was completed, I wanted to call it *Molly Minion's Most Remarkable Life*, because she is such an extraordinary woman, with an incredible life story, but Molly insisted that her experiences were no more remarkable than that of any other person, so ultimately I lost the debate, and we settled simply on the title, *Molly's Memoir*.

With this being said, I will now introduce you to Ms. Molly Minion, and her sidekick, Allison, and I will meet up with you in two shakes of a sheep's tail.

Best Regards,
Carolyn

Springfield Senior Care Facility
1990
"The Noisy Neighbor"

Molly carefully balanced her teacup in one hand as she attempted to slide the stiff patio door open with her free hand. The petite veranda outside her tiny apartment at Springfield Senior Care Facility provided adequate shade in the mornings and offered breathtaking views of the mountains at sunset. Molly plopped down onto the wrought iron chair, took a long sip of the Earl Grey tea, and grinned knowingly when she spied a tiny sparrow on the limb of an oak tree, only two feet away. The early morning colors were hazy in the soft mist, causing her spirit to drift back to the dense woods in the highlands of West Virginia.

I sing because I'm happy,
I sing because I'm free.
For His eye is on the sparrow,
And I know He watches me.

"Good morning, Molly," she heard her neighbor's blaring greeting.

Molly startled, then frowned, when she saw the sparrow flutter away. She briefly wondered why Allison was always so noisy and boisterous. *"She must be the loudest woman I have met in my entire lifetime, and I ended up right next door to her."* She unconsciously drummed her fingers on the tabletop. *"It is troubling how life turns out sometimes."* Molly awkwardly twisted in her seat to face the other woman. "It is a glorious day," she kindly replied.

"Indeed, it is. I always rise early in the morning, 'cause my midnight oil is all used up by nine o'clock." Allison nodded wistfully, "Do you have grand plans for this morning?"

"Nothing particular," Molly replied. "I thought I might enjoy the *quiet* peacefulness that accompanies sunrise each morning," she provided a pointed glance toward the other woman. Unfortunately, it went unnoticed.

"I agree completely. There is nothing like a little quiet time in the morning," as soon as the words escaped her mouth, Allison started hacking and coughing viciously. "Sorry," she yelled out after the fit had passed, "allergies." She raucously scooted her chair backward and walked over to the tiny fence dividing the two living areas. "I have been wondering, Molly, exactly how old are you?"

"I don't really know," Molly silently considered.

"The reason I ask, is because you are practically wrinkle-free, and it made me think that maybe you have some African American blood in your line. Do you?"

"I don't have a clue," she disregarded Allison's assumption.

"I do declare, it seems to me that African American women don't get all wrinkled up like other women our age. The Lord only knows how much facial cream I've applied throughout my years, and it didn't seem to help all that much. Although, I did see a new product advertised in Ladies Home Journal and it guarantees that I can look ten years younger in only two weeks. I aim to order some." She paused and took in a deep breath, "Not that it matters much anymore. Since my husband passed away I don't have a lot of reason to worry about what I look like. To tell you the truth, these days my main squeeze is Charmin." She shook her head as her lips pursed together, "Did you ever get married?" Without allowing time for Molly to reply she continued, "I don't know if you've paid much mind to it, but there's not one decent bachelor residing at the Springfield Senior Care Facility." She seemed to ponder her own statement before expounding. "But, that is probably because women live longer than men, wouldn't you say?"

Molly stared expressionless at the other woman, wondering exactly which of the previous questions she should attempt to illuminate upon.

Obviously not requiring any response at all, Allison carried on with the one-sided conversation. "Where do you call home, Molly? I notice a slight southern twang in your voice," she juddered her finger teasingly in the air. "But, of course, having lived all over the country, I could distinguish a southern accent even if my ears were stuffed full of cotton."

Ears stuffed full of cotton, sounds like a grand idea. Do I have any cotton in the bathroom cabinet? Realizing that stuffing cotton into her ears to mute the sound of the blabbering neighbor was unrealistic, not to mention rude, she sighed deeply before asking the animated woman if she would like to join her for a cup of tea.

"I would *love* to. Thank you so much for asking. I really should be cleaning my apartment today, but I'm so far over my head, I'd have to look up to see my bottom." She shrugged her shoulders dismissively, "So why bother?" Allison let out a roaring laugh as she shamelessly hiked up her dress to her waist, providing Molly with an unwanted view of her tight knee-high hose and oversized bloomers, before tossing her leg over the railing. "You are so very kind to invite me for tea." She pulled up a chair and collapsed onto the plush cushion, as Molly went inside to gather the teapot, cookies, and a spare cup.

When she returned, she gently placed the tray on the table, "Please help yourself, Allison."

"Thank you, very much." Allison popped two biscotti cookies into her mouth before informing her neighbor. "I just love these cookies. They just dissolve right on your tongue. This is a fine treat, Molly." She offered up a half smile, "Do you know the other night I sunk my teeth into a steak and they stayed there?" She sighed dramatically before inquiring, "So, Molly, you didn't tell me. Where *exactly* did you grow up?"

Taking advantage of the fact that Allison's mouth was stuffed full, Molly figured she had a couple of seconds to talk, so she settled on sharing some of the noteworthy events that she had experienced during her eighty-odd years here on earth.

Honestly, the authenticity of her *entire* story cannot be verified, but these are Molly's memories, along with tales she had been told, which together, have formed a most remarkable life.

Monongahela Mountains, West Virginia
October 23, 1905

Mr. Minion pushed open the door of the cabin and immediately froze when he heard the shrilling sound of an infant crying. He knew, for sure, that when he'd left out this morning there weren't any babies living with him, and as far as he could recollect, he wasn't expecting none either.

"Nina?" He called out as he hung his coat on a nail by the door, "Is everything alright in here?"

Nina motioned for him to join her behind the patchwork blanket that served as the partition between their sleeping areas, "Come over here, Mr. Minion. You ain't gonna believe what got left on our doorstep this morning while I was out gathering berries." She carefully picked up the child and with her free hand unwrapped the cloth that was tucked in tight around the baby's face.

"What is it?" Mr. Minion asked as he stared at the child.

"What do you think it is?" Nina looked at him pointedly.

"A baby?"

"You're sure full of your wits today, Mr. Minion."

His gaze darted from the baby, to the woman, and back to the youngin' again. "What are we gonna do with it?"

Nina pressed her lips together then released a hushed sigh before replying, "What would any good Christian do with a child that God delivered to their door?" Her brow arched as she awaited his response.

"Do you mean to tell me that somebody just left a baby on our doorstep?"

"Yes, indeed."

He paused briefly as he took in the news, "Well, I guess it was better than puttin' it in a basket and floatin' it down the river like little Moses."

"Yes, it was definitely a better choice considering the size of the rapids in the river today," Nina agreed. "There's gonna be a gully washer down in the valley this evening, I expect."

Mr. Minion stretched over to rub the child's chubby nose, "Is it a boy or a girl?"

"It's a little girl," Nina told him, as her face crinkled with pleasure.

"She's sure a sight for sore eyes," Mr. Minion mumbled, "but she don't smell very good."

Nina shook her head as she glared at Mr. Minion in disbelief, "She needs her cloth changed, she's soiled herself." Nina handed the child over into the lumbering man's arms, "You hold on to her for a bit while I slit some soft material to make a diaper." She started rummaging through a wooden chest that held potato sacks, remnants of old material, and clothing beyond repair. She pulled out a timeworn cotton shirt from the bottom of the box, picked up a knife, and slit the cloth into smaller pieces. She lifted up the pot of steaming water from the old coal stove and poured some into a bucket.

Nina noticed Mr. Minion holding the child out at arms length as he studied the little one inquisitively. "She ain't gonna bite you, Mr. Minion, she ain't got no teeth yet. Hold her close to your chest so she won't be afraid."

Mr. Minion pulled the child close to his trunk and awkwardly adjusted the blanket that was tucked around her, and as he did, a dark brown stream trickled onto his arm and slowly oozed down toward his hand. "Oh, Lord.

Nina!" He began to gag uncontrollably, "I think I'm gonna be poorly."

"Mr. Minion," she propped her hand on her hip, "you just gutted a deer and you're gonna get poorly when a child soils your arm a bit?" She once again shook her head as she pulled the baby from his arms and rested her on the table. "I hope you properly saved the deer's hide to tan," she murmured under her breath as she proceeded to dip a smooth cloth into a bucket of warm water. She held it there for a moment, before pulling it out and twisting it tightly to wring out the water.

Mr. Minion walked over to the table, hastily snatched up the portion of cloth Nina had discarded, and intently scrubbed at his arm as he watched the woman expertly scrub the child, from head to toe, before tying a triangular cloth around her bottom. She gently smoothed the russet curls on the baby's head, hoisted her up to her shoulder, and commenced to rhythmically pat the youngster on the back.

"Her colorin' is a little funny, don't ya think, Nina?"

"Her colorin' is funny? What in the tarnation are you talkin' about?" Nina's stare sharpened, "Do ya think it is funnier than your frosty hue and snowy white beard? Or ya think it's funnier than my red-tinted skin and coal black braid?"

Mr. Minion continued to gape at the little girl, "I don't know, Nina. It's just different. Not the same as either one of ours. That's all I meant – you don't need to get all riled up."

Nina ignored Mr. Minion and started humming softly as she rocked the baby back and forth in her arms.

"Nina," Mr. Minion stared at the woman for a right long

spell before offering up, "maybe we should get married and raise this little one together." He gulped back the lump that was forming in his throat, "I've always wanted to have a child."

"Considerin' the way your kind treated my ancestors, I figure they wouldn't be too fond of me weddin' a white man," she replied without looking him straight in the eye. "They'd probably spit down at us from the sky."

"I'm red sometimes," he mumbled, "especially when I work out in the sun too long."

"That's a different kind of red."

"Well, you wouldn't have to tell your ancestors the whole truth. You could just say that you were going to marry a good man who is red in the summertime." He gave her a sly wink, "What do ya say? You know I'm fancy for ya."

Nina glanced down at the chubby cheeked child again before directing her attention toward Mr. Minion. "You're a fine man." She paused momentarily, "I reckon I'm quite smitten with you, too."

"Is that a yes, Nina?" His cheeks deepened to slashes as his mouth turned up at the corners.

"Yes." Nina gave him a sincere smile, "It's a yes."

Mr. Minion walked around the table and gave Nina a tight hug before spiritedly slapping her behind.

She swatted at his hand, "Well I'll be, Mr. Minion! You best get that preacher up here before you start taking those kind of liberties."

He chuckled. "I'll go fetch him right now," he added a wink of his eye.

Mr. Minion proceeded to rub his bulky, rough finger gently over the baby's chin, "What are we gonna call her?"

"How about Molly?" Nina suggested, "It's a good

American name."

"Molly Minion," the man repeated. "It is the most beautiful name I've ever heard." He scratched at his beard for a second, "I think I'll have her call me Pop."

"Pop?" Nina repeated. "It has a nice sound to it," she nodded her head approvingly. "I just might start calling you Pop, too."

"That'd be fine by me. You can call me anything you want, just don't call me late for supper," he laughed as he walked toward the door. Mr. Minion grabbed his coat and opened the door with intentions of calling on the preacher, but as soon as he stepped outside he saw a man riding a horse up the path. The man started shouting before he even got to the porch, "Is Ms. Nina here? My wife is in labor and is having an awful time. She told me to ride up here and fetch her. It's bad."

Nina could clearly overhear the conversation going on outside, so she grabbed her overstuffed brown satchel, settled her favorite battered leather hat on her head, and scurried out the door. She shoved little Molly into Mr. Minion's arms and hurdled up onto the back of the man's saddle.

"I'll be back shortly," she yelled over her shoulder, "Pop."

"Nina," Mr. Minion hollered back, "don't be bringin' no more children home 'til we get this one half raised. Okay?"

Nina pretended she didn't hear him, but she was grinnin' like a possum eatin' persimmons as the horse took off galloping down the steep mountain path.

Springfield Senior Care Facility
1990
"Tall Tales"

"I am flabbergasted! Are you telling me that an Indian midwife and a mountain man in the hills of West Virginia raised you? You sure can spin a tale, Molly." Allison teased as she polished off the last biscotti cookie and clanked her empty cup down hard on the tabletop. "My dear departed husband and I visited Seneca Rock years ago. That's in the same area, isn't it?" Allison scrunched her brow tight as if trying to recall, "Yes, I do believe it is."

Molly nodded. "Yes, it's very close to..."

Allison interjected, "It is one of the tallest points in West Virginia, right? I do remember now." She smacked her leg pretentiously, "Is it the highest peak in the Allegheny Mountains? I'll tell you one thing, it is colder than a well-diggers butt up there." She peeped sideways toward Molly, "My husband liked to vacation in the most unusual places, I never could figure out why. I used to ask him, 'Why don't we just go to Myrtle Beach, like the rest of the world?' But, he would always say he wanted to go somewhere quiet and peaceful. I never could figure him out. Men are funny, aren't they?"

"He probably fantasized of going somewhere peaceful because you talked his leg off," Molly thought.

Allison obliviously didn't wait for her reply, "I don't recall if I ever told you, but my husband was a private detective, and he was a sweet-talking thing. He used to travel all over the country looking for folks or finding out other people's secrets, and I would always go with him. He said me tagging along helped with his," she wiggled her fingers in the air indicating quotation marks, "undercover disguise." She peeked at Molly to see if she was still listening, "It made him look inconspicuous with me by his side. You wouldn't believe how sneaky people are, Molly." She shook her head in disgust, "But, he could find a needle in a haystack and I sure learned a few of his tricks over the years. For example, I can always tell when someone is trying to pull the wool over my eyes." She pointed her finger at Molly, "Have you ever met Mrs. Johnson who lives four doors down? I swear she couldn't tell the truth if she was reading straight from the Good Book." Allison paused to consider for a second before confiding, "Of course, she may be getting senile." She bobbed her head up and down a few times before heaving a long, drawn-out, sigh. "It sure is peaceful out here this morning. Don't you think?"

"Relative to what?" Molly considered, *"An atomic bomb exploding? A plane crash?"*

"Why don't you tell me some more about growing up in the mountains?" Her eyes sparkled with enthusiasm as she stared at the other woman, "I could just plant myself, right here, and listen to your stories all day long. It's so amazing!" She shot her a sincere glance, "If you want to know the truth, my life has been rather uneventful and dull."

A sad expression suddenly crossed Allison's face, "How about I go fix us a couple of Bloody Mary's and we'll visit for a little longer?" She rose from her chair, sauntered over to the fence, hiked up her skirt, and launched her leg over the top. "I'll be right back," she assured.

"I have no doubt," Molly mused.

Monongahela Mountains, West Virginia
March 14, 1907

"That girl's livelier than a puppy with two tails," Pop Minion announced to Nina as he slammed the hoe down hard into the earth.

"That she is," Nina agreed, dropping a seed potato down into the fresh soil. "I hope we can get most of these planted before that rain starts in again." Nina glanced up at the sky before tossing a few more seedlings on the ground. She paused and took a look around to check on Molly. When she didn't see her anywhere a wave of panic enveloped her. "Where is the child, Pop? Do ya see her?"

Pop scanned the garden as Nina started slowly walking toward the woods. "Molly?" she called out. "Molly?" Nina could hear a distant scrunching in the woods down by the river, and started walking in that direction. She suddenly heard a scream, followed by the clamor of someone sliding recklessly down the mountain. She took off running toward the river, with Pop following behind, right on her heels.

When Nina reached the bank of the raging stream, she could see swirls of white foam and debris gushing downstream in the gray-green water, and she felt the wet leaves cold and limp underfoot. The roar of the river was deafening and caused her heart to beat faster as she frantically scanned the plunging water in the ravine. Maybe her imagination was tricking her, but in the murky gloom over there, she thought she saw a figure floating downstream among the tree trunks. The trees in the bank stood high out of the sand, their grotesque, gnarled root boles two or three feet above the ground where the soil had washed out from under them. *"There she is,"* Nina was sure of it now. Her little girl was caught up in the rushing river, and the fast stream was gurglingly chaotically as she haphazardly made her way over the rain-slick rock slabs at the river's edge.

After a short while, breathing hard, she gave up chasing the child down the riverside and Pop Minion watched in horror as Nina leapt, feet first, into the rushing stream. He could see Nina's dark black braid floating on top of the water and her hand grasping hold of little Molly's head, pulling it up high above the rapids by the hair on her head. He saw her clutching, with her free hand, at tree roots as they hurtled downstream. For a moment it seemed as if her fingertips had caught hold of a cold, wet rock but the motion of a log smacking into her back dislodged her grip.

The rumbling, hissing force of the plummeting water was pounding Nina's sense into a state of disorientation as she bobbed her head up to catch a deep breath, hoping the cleansing air would give her a moment to think.

Pop could still see them, now twenty-feet farther down the turbulent ravine. Nina's braid was still floating on top of the water's crest, but her head was nowhere to be seen. Her left hand desperately searching for something to grasp hold of, her right holding the child's face above the water's cutting edge. "No!" He cried out as he took off running along the side of the riverbed. "Hold on, Nina! I'm right behind ya. Grab ahold of something – anything!" He screamed. *"How long can she hold her breath? Has it been over six minutes now? Was that her head I just saw above the water line?"* He counted seconds as he followed their floating bodies down the ravine. He spied Nina's left hand as it exploded from beneath the raging stream again. Her fingers gripped a snarled limb of a tree trunk. He rushed, panicking, to where she was desperately trying to keep hold, and submerged his arm, blindly grappling through the muddy water.

Nina felt the water roaring ominously behind her and caught sight of the little girl's head that was still above the raging water. She forced herself up, gasped for air, and slid back into the furious river. The bole of the tree felt as though it was shifting. She repositioned her hand, determined not to release it – not yet. Not until she had to.

She felt a strong hand wrap around her wrist, as she frantically tightened her fingers trying to secure the grip.

Within a split-second, Pop plucked them from the water and threw them, in a heap, onto the wet sand. All six-foot-five inches and three hundred fifty pounds plopped down on top of them.

Little Molly's face was a mask of crying terror as the water spurted out from her lungs.

They lay there a long time trembling. Pop kept whimpering, over and over again, "Thank you, God! Thank you, God! Thank you, my sweet Lord!" When the sudden realization of all that he had almost lost fully hit him, his body began to convulse. Pure wails of thankfulness leapt from his heart. He held his family tight to his chest, as he wept uncontrollably, his chest deeply expanding and subsiding with each breath. His large, oversized body remained on top of Nina and Molly, providing a blanket of protection from the rain that was now pelting down from the skies.

Several long moments had passed before Pop's breathing started to calm down.

Nina nudged at his shoulder, "Pop?"
"Yes, Nina?"
"You're squashin' us."

Springfield Senior Care Facility
1990
"Kindred Spirits"

"I remember that flood. Well, I remember my mama talking about it, anyway." Allison squinted her eyes as if trying to pull back a distant memory, "We were living in Ohio at the time, and if I remember correctly, the rivers all over West Virginia, Ohio, and Pennsylvania rose and washed out all kinds of homes and businesses. I think there were several folks who drowned, too." She glanced at Molly, "God's angels were sure enough watching over you, huh?"

Molly nodded in agreement.

Allison continued on, "I vaguely recollect sitting in a little boat with my papa and brother and rowing right smack-dab down the middle of Main Street in Portsmouth, Ohio. That kind of thing is something that just sticks with you. We were just floating along looking through the windows of the department stores." Her eyes popped wide open, as though something important had just occurred to her, "Can you believe we were both caught up in the very same flood in 1907?" She took a long sip of her beverage, "And now we are best friends, just sitting here enjoying a Bloody Mary together."

"Best friends?" Molly ruminated on the fact that today was the first time they had engaged in a conversation.

"Do you know the flood is probably the last memory I have of my papa, because he died just a few months after, and then we all moved in with Grandma Thorne."

Molly noticed a sadness creep across the other woman's

face again. It appeared that an uninvited memory had forcibly pushed its way into her thoughts. Allison stared at the bright red pot of geraniums blankly for a few seconds before soliciting, "Tell me another story about West Virginia, Molly. Would you?"

Allison plucked the stalk of celery from her glass and chomped down on it, as Molly recollected a glimmer of one of the most unsettling events in her life.

Monongahela Mountains, West Virginia
March 19, 1909

Nina was busy kneading dough, while Molly sat on the rough, oak plank floor of the cabin, singing and sorting through the spring wildflowers. She was plucking out the dandelions, and delicately placing them into a neat pile beside her basket, so Nina could dry them out later to brew tea.

Pop lumbered through the doorway and pecked Nina's cheek before he squatted down in the middle of the floor to play with Molly.

"How was your day, Pop?" Nina asked as she massaged the sticky bread gently.

"I had a fine day, Nina. I'm sorry I didn't get more done around the farm, but the barn raising over at the Osborne's took longer than I expected."

"No problem, Pop." She sprinkled a handful of flour on the wooden counter.

"Mrs. Osborne gave me a couple gifts for the two special girls in my life." He grinned.

"Is that right?" Nina glanced over her shoulder.

He slid a porcelain doll out of a brown paper poke and presented it to the little girl. "I have something special for you, Molly."

Molly studied the doll curiously as her face beamed with joy. The doll didn't look like Nina, or like Pop. The beautiful doll, with an auburn lace trimmed dress, and russet-colored hair reminded Molly of what she looked like when she stared into Nina's hand-held mirror. Her skin was the exact same color as the brown eggs Nina would gather from the chicken coop. "Is this for me?"

"Yep," Pop was so proud he could hardly contain his excitement. "It is your very own. You can name her anything you'd like."

Molly grinned from ear to ear, as she bounced to her feet to offer him a hug. "Thank you, Pop. She's so pretty. I love you."

"I love you, too."

Molly noticed a hairline crack just below the doll's knee. She didn't care. She had banged her knees so frequently that she figured the fancy doll must have fallen down in the briar patch, just like she had done so many times.

"And," Pop announced as he puffed up, "I have a gift for Nina."

"For me?" Nina scolded. "Pop, you don't need to give me nothing. I have everything I need."

"Well," he rubbed his shortly trimmed beard, "I have something for ya, anyway." He reached in his pocket and pulled out a tiny brooch, covered with green stones that put him in mind of the color of newly budding trees in springtime. "It's a pin." He handed it to Nina. "Mrs. Osborne called it something fancy… a broke … no, a brotch … a brooch. That's what she called it, a brooch. Ya can pin it on your shirt."

Nina's face beamed as she asked Pop to attach it to her faded suede tunic. "Thank you, Pop. It is lovely." She gave him a big hug, careful to not smear the flour dough on his shirt.

"I've been thinking, Pop." Nina said as she turned back to her chore. "I heard there was a used steam-powered tractor for plowing at Jack's Hardware Store over in

Whitmer. You should take a trip down there and see if it's any good. It sure would help out with the chores around the farm, plus you wouldn't have to work so hard. I worry about you."

"We can't afford a fancy tractor. Besides, I don't mind hard work. I'd work my fingers to the bone to keep you and little Molly happy. I don't mind at all." He added sincerely, "Really."

Nina's head tilted toward the cluster of glassware on the countertop, "Pop, we do have the money. I heard the tractor was selling for three-hundred dollars, and we have three-hundred and twenty dollars right there in the Ball Jar."

"What Ball Jar?" Pop asked confused.

"The blue one. Right there," she directed his attention using a spoon as her pointer.

"Where did we get that much money?"

Nina nonchalantly replied, "You know I make money as a midwife, and selling my herbs, so I trade, sell, and barter with folks for things we need. For example, a couple weeks ago Mr. Jameson gave me a whole set of crystal dishes, which we don't need, so I sold them to Gabriel Wheeler." She devoted a quick wave to the sky, "The Lord takes good care of us, Pop."

"That He does," Pop admitted. "I'll sleep on it."

"Well, ya best get there before somebody else buys it. Besides, you know as well as I do that we hit rocks all over the fields when we are planting. It would make it easier for both of us."

Pop stared at the blue Ball jar as he thought-out Nina's proposal. "I'll take the wagon to town in the morning and see what's what."

Nina nodded approvingly, "Can ya take Molly with you?

I need to call on the Jameson family in the morning to check up on their little girl."

Early the following morning, before the rooster had even risen, Pop filled the lamplight with oil, hitched the horses to the wagon, and tucked a quilt over Molly's legs, before they headed out for the long drive to the town of Whitmer. They traveled down the lengthy, narrow path, across a shallow creek bed, then up the worn dirt trail surrounded by parting trees. Pop was singing, as he so often did, when they approached the brick buildings marking the south side of the city of Whitmer.

I sing because I'm happy,
I sing because I'm free.
For His eye is on the sparrow,
And I know He watches me.

They passed the post office and a dry goods store before he slowed the horses pace. The sun was barely rising, as he scanned the dim street for a place to secure the reins. Pop spied Jack's Hardware Store, noticing a light burning brightly through the window, and began to steer the horses into an alley alongside the aged, wooden building.

"What's that man doing?" Molly suddenly asked Pop.

"What man?"

Molly pointed toward a man who was dangling from a flagpole, a noose around his neck. His inanimate body was limp and lifeless and Molly noticed he had lost a shoe. "Why ain't he wearin' both of his shoes, Pop?"

"Whoa," Pop pulled tightly on the horses bit. He stopped and stared disbelievingly for a long moment. He began to panic. *"A lynching,"* Pop recognized in horror. The terror he felt as he gaped at the man encircled him, as he forced back the bile that had risen into his throat. "Oh, God. Oh, Lord." Pop's voice was quivering. "Molly, get down, cover yourself up with the quilt, and don't make a sound." He pulled to the right on the bit collar, in an attempt to redirect the horses before speeding up their gait.

Pop's heart was thumping faster than the horses could bolt, as the sun peeked over the foothill, fully exposing the transgressions that had previously been shielded in the gloomy shadows, of the once innocent town of Whitmer.

Springfield Senior Care Facility
1990
"Wild and Wooly"

Allison's jaw fell open, as her wide eyes stared at Molly. "A lynching? How horrible! Did you ever learn the details?"

Molly sipped at her Bloody Mary, "Nina and Pop talked about the incident on many occasions over the years. Apparently, about fifty to one hundred masked men entered the jail where a man named Joe Brown was being held for the murder of the Chief of Police. They took him from his cell and strung him up on a flagpole. Brown was a notorious character who had earned the reputation as an outlaw. He had cut his wife's throat, murdered two United States Marshals, and served several terms in various prisons and penitentiaries. A real mean man."

Allison grasped the pitcher full of tomato juice and poured herself another drink. "You must have been terrified," she said as she splashed a drop of Tabasco into her glass.

"Actually, I didn't understand what was happening, but when Pop started trembling I knew something was wrong. I remember when Pop directed me to hide under the quilt, I had glanced at the street and saw the man's missing shoe lying in the mud. Pop placed his hand on my head and pulled the quilt over me. When the tears started streaming down my cheeks, I covered my mouth with my hands so my cries couldn't be heard. I was shaking all the way home."

"So, it wasn't a hate crime." Allison assumed.

Molly shrugged her shoulders. "It was a hate crime of

sorts, I suppose." She motioned for Allison to pour her another one. "Nina insisted her kin dealt with mean folks in a similar manner. Be it right, or be it wrong."

Allison leaned forward on her elbows, her green eyes intent with attention, absorbed by her words. "Still," she whistled softly, "what an appalling event to witness."

Molly agreed, "I can still envision the man hanging from the pole, as if it took place only yesterday. It was an incident I will never forget."

"West Virginia was sure wild and wooly back then, eh?"

"It was for sure." Molly said, as she floated back in time to the day when the rangers arrived.

Monongahela Mountains, West Virginia
June 20, 1915

Nina had just finished weaving her thick dark hair into a long braid that snaked down her back to her hips, the stray wisps left drifting around her chin. She picked up a knife and had just begun to demonstrate to Molly how she needed the apples to be peeled for the cider they were planning to make, when they heard a parade of horses climbing the mountain. Nina snatched up her rifle, opened the front door, stepped out onto the porch and cocked the shotgun. She motioned to Molly to prop open the window and handed her the spare rifle. The six men riding on horses halted a few yards away. Molly waited for the door to slap shut before she snuck over, cracked open the window, and slid the slim cask through the tiny gap.

"What can I help you gentlemen with this afternoon?" Nina asked, as the long metal barrel steered a few feet above their heads.

"We're United States Rangers and the federal government has assigned us to inform you folks about a land offer we have for ya," the man wearing a dirty black hat and shiny boots replied.

"I assure you we don't need no federal government offers," Nina glared at him as she thought back over the turmoil her people had suffered due to government propositions.

"Is this your land?" A younger man with fire-red hair inquired.

"Sure is." Nina curtly responded.

She overheard him murmur, "I didn't think Indians were allowed to own land."

"What did you say, Mister?" Yeah, that's what she thought. A racist. She lowered her aim toward his hat. "If I recall history correctly, this land belonged to my kin, way before the white men stole it away."

"Shut up, Jack." One of the other men scolded. "He didn't mean anything, Ma'am. The federal government has passed, what is titled, the Weeks Act and they are buying land from willing sellers at a fair market price. We are here to offer your family four dollars and fifteen cents an acre for your property. The government is eager to buy up this forest and preserve it." The man spit tobacco juice on the ground, "They're planning on turning this entire area into a national park, and provide watershed protection," he continued as be commenced to dismount. "According to the deeds and witness trees, your family owns about five-hundred acres."

"Five-hundred and four acres," she corrected. "You best stay put on that horse," Nina's eyes narrowed.

"I just have some papers I want ya to read," the man held up a brown envelope to show her.

"Drop it on the ground," she motioned with the barrel of her gun. "Me and my husband will take a look at 'em later."

Nina couldn't believe the man continued to get down from his mount. *"Is he deaf or downright ignorant?"*

From inside the cabin, Molly could see the man dismounting, even though Nina had told him to drop the papers. His actions sent an unswerving wave of panic through her body. *"If you ever feel someone is threatening me, or your Pop, I want ya to aim this gun straight up into the clouds and pull the trigger. Okay?"* Molly recalled Nina practicing this with her many times.

So, Molly fired a shot, up high into the heavens. The pop of a firecracker, and the smell of acrid black smoke, caused the young girl to tremble, but when she noticed Nina hadn't even flinched, she held strong and steady.

The unexpected explosion made the man balk for a brief second before repositioning himself back on the saddle, all the time trying to disguise the startled expression in his eyes.

Nina deliberately wrapped her finger around the trigger, broadened her stance, and secured her footing.

He tossed an envelope on the dirt, as a diverting grin spanned his face.

"Your business is done here," Nina glared. "Which means that you have three minutes to get off my land."

"But..."

Nina confidently wielded her weapon. "Two minutes," she calmly articulated.

"Yes, Ma'am." With a slight nod of his head and a snap of his heel, the man directed his horse to turn, as his companions followed quickly, and silently, behind.

"Don't be comin' back up here," Nina yelled, "we'll get in touch with you if we're interested."

She could see the young man with fire-red hair shaking erratically, as he admitted to the others, "I think I just pissed my britches."

"You ain't the only one, Jack." The man sporting the shiny boots confessed.

Springfield Care Facility
1990
"Promises"

"Well, I do declare," Allison remarked, "I don't think I have ever heard of the Weeks Act. Was it for real or were they trying to swindle your family?"

"Oh, it was a legitimate act signed into law by President William Howard Taft back in 1911, and it basically permitted the federal government to purchase private land to protect the rivers and watersheds in the eastern United States." Molly informed her friend, "It was an important and successful piece of conservation legislation."

"So, your family didn't have to sell out?"

"No," Molly polished off her drink and delicately positioned her glass on the tabletop, "only the folks who wanted to sell. Obviously Nina and Pop had no interest in moving away from the farm, so they never contacted the rangers after Nina rushed them off the mountain."

Allison twisted open the top of a bottle of pimento cheese and spread some on a cracker before offering it to Molly, "Well, at least they didn't boot ya out of your home."

Molly graciously accepted the cheese-covered cracker and popped it into her mouth. "No," she mused as she considered Nina's rants and raves concerning the treatment of American Indians, "it wasn't the same type of deal they offered to the Native Americans. Nina held a profound mistrust of the government, and said she would just as soon 'shoot 'em full of buckshot, as to listen to their promises'."

"Was it true that Indians weren't allowed to own land

back then?"

Molly confirmed this bit of history, "During this particular time in history, they were not. What is so interesting is that Seneca women held sole ownership of all the home and land, and inheritance and property descended through the maternal line. It was the women who were in charge of their clans."

"Really?" Allison laughed, "Nina sure was a firecracker, wasn't she?"

"For sure," Molly fondly recalled Nina's stories. "I think it was inherited. Nina said if the 'clan mothers' didn't agree with any major decisions made by the chiefs, who were men, they would eventually depose them."

Allison reflected on this briefly, "Do you mean they would simply overthrow them?"

"Yep."

"I guess the Seneca Indian women were raised to be strong, and Nina must have passed it down to you."

"Oh," Molly dismissed her assumption, "I'm not nearly as strong as Nina was, I can assure you."

"I wish I would have lived somewhere exciting when I was growing up." Allison considered her family's moving into the modest home of her grandparents in a small town in Ohio. Her mama had promised them a better life, but instead they doubled-up in the beds, didn't have enough food to fill their bellies, and she spent the years holding her breath, just waiting for her grandfather to start screaming and cussing, or worse. She banished the thought from her mind. "So, what else do you remember about living with Nina and Pop?"

Monongahela Mountains, West Virginia
May 26, 1916

Molly took off down the mountain, in search of blackberries and other edibles she might find in the woods. She was using a long pointed stick to clear the path, just in case the snakes were out looking for berries, too. The further she walked down the mountain, the steamier it got, and by the time she made it to the witness tree that marked the edge of their land, perspiration was dripping from almost every pore of her body.

"The spring weather in the mountains is so fickle," she reasoned, *"and today the heat and humidity is as hot as burning coals."* The thick air made Molly feel lethargic, like she could use a good, long nap. She dropped down under the big white oak and collapsed on the mossy grass. She could spy, through slices between the branches, the dense white clouds sluggishly drifting by and she figured the clouds were moving slow 'cause of the thickness in the air, too. She felt just like the puffs in the sky today, sleepy, listless and lazy.

Molly closed her eyes and wished a good strong mountain breeze would knock through, to cool her off a bit. She was about to drift off when she heard a scrunching of leaves, followed by a sudden voice that compelled her to dart straight up.

"What ya doing down here?" A boy's voice quietly asked.

"It ain't none of your business," Molly looked him over, "who are you? This is our property. This white oak is our witness tree, so you shouldn't be around here."

"This here is our witness tree, too." The young man set his chin. "The land on this side of the tree belongs to our family."

"And who is *your* family?" Molly inquired suspiciously.

"My name is Zach Moore," he informed her, "I'm the youngest son in the family."

"Oh," Molly tilted her head, "well, it's nice to meet ya, Zach Moore. I'm Molly Minion."

"Pleased to make your acquaintance."

"Likewise."

"So, what ya doin' so far down the mountain?"

"I'm out gathering some berries," she fanned her face with her hand, "but, it's so dag-on hot today I laid down for a minute to rest."

"It is hotter than blue blazes, for sure." He pointed his finger up toward the big oak tree, "I came down to see if I could spy some flying squirrels, 'cause I love watching those little varmints."

Molly glimpsed up at the tree. "I hadn't paid much mind to them. They kinda look like bats with tails to me."

Zach grinned and nodded his head, "That's what makes them so much fun to watch. They mostly come out at night," he informed her, "but sometimes you can see 'em in the day if you watch close in the shadows."

"Yeah, I suppose." Molly considered briefly, "I'd rather watch the clouds float by. Look there!" She pointed to a clearing between the limbs of the tree, "There goes a big ole sparrow right now, do ya see it?"

"Where's it at?" Zach squinted his eyes, as he followed the direction of Molly's finger. "Well, I'll be," he acknowledged, "there is a big ole sparrow in the sky."

They grinned contently as they watched the sparrow

change forms and slowly drift out of sight.

"Hey, Molly. Let me ask ya something."

"Sure," she shrugged her shoulders, "what do ya want to know?"

"Is Nina your mama?"

With narrowed eyes, Molly studied him prudently before responding, "That's a silly question, Zach Moore. Of course, Nina's my mama." Molly propped her hand on her hip, "Why would ya ask me somethin' like that?"

"You don't look like Nina, that's all." He peeked at her sideways before adding, "You don't look like Mr. Minion either. You look more akin to the folks that live up Tucker Holler." He casually spit on the ground, "Everyone in my family looks alike. We all have red hair and freckles, so I just figured your family might not be blood kin." He added further clarification, "'Cause ya don't look like your folks."

Molly didn't reply. She didn't know what to say. She hadn't given it much thought. Not until this very moment. She glanced down to her dark hand and thought about Nina's long, straight black hair and Pop's white beard. "*I better bring this up at supper,*" she figured.

The boy pulled a black walnut from his pocket, "Would ya care for a nut?"

Molly peeped at his offering, "I don't much care for them 'cause they stain my fingers black."

"Not if ya crack 'em open with a knife," he explained as he clicked open the dull blade of his pocketknife. He expertly demonstrated the proper technique for shelling a walnut, pried the nutmeat loose, and handed it to her.

She nibbled on the nut as he continued to crack another one open.

Zach and Molly chomped on the treats as they watched a

squirrel glide from branch to branch above them.

"Well," she released a hushed sigh, "I best be heading back up the mountain before Nina starts lookin' for me. It was nice meeting you, Zach Moore, and thanks for the nuts."

"You too, Molly. Maybe I'll see ya down here again and we can squirrel watch some more."

"Maybe," Molly told the boy, "I come down 'bout every day after I finish up my chores."

"Molly," Zach stretched his hand out and touched her shoulder, "I didn't mean nothin' bad about your family. I was just wonderin'."

"I didn't take no offense," she fibbed.

Molly studied on Zach's remark, all the way back up to the top of the mountain.

As soon as the girl reached the flat spot of the highland, she could see Nina crouched down next to the barn shucking ears of corn. She was tossing the husks to the side as quickly as she dropped the cobs into a pot of salt water.

"Molly, go get washed up and ready for supper. Pop's already in the cabin and all we need to finish up is boiling this corn and slicing up some tomatoes."

"Do ya want me to tend to the tomatoes?" Molly asked.

"Scrub your hands first," Nina replied without looking up.

Molly let the door slap shut behind her and cleaned her hands with lye soap and warm water. She angrily plopped a tomato on the table, noticing it split on impact, and began chopping the vegetable into thin slices. She was still thinkin' on what Zach Moore had asked her when they were down at the witness tree, and she had all intentions of finding out the truth. *Right after Pop says grace, I'm gonna just straight-out ask 'em."*

"Are you alright, Molly?" Pop asked as he placed the drinking jars on the table.

"I'm fine," Molly replied flatly.

"You sure don't seem fine." Pop scratched at his beard, "Do ya have something stuck in your craw?"

"Do I have something stuck in my craw?" Molly rolled her eyes dramatically, *"Maybe you ain't my daddy, and Nina ain't my mama, and nobody cared enough to let me know?"* She slammed the knife she was using hard down on the table. "No, I'm just fine," she repeated.

She swooshed open the door, crossed her arms in front of her chest, stubbornly walked out to the long, low porch, sat down on a wooden chair and stared out at the hillside that was bursting bright blooms of yellow, purple, and red. Molly noticed stray whirlybirds twirling down from the maple tree, and a groundhog scurrying through the shady woods, only a few feet away. She intentionally ignored Nina when she walked across the wooden porch and awkwardly opened the door with her free hand while balancing the pot of corn in her other hand.

A few minutes later, Nina cracked the door open and announced, "Supper's ready."

Molly disconcertedly shuffled in and dropped down by the table. Nina and Pop glanced sideways at each other, each of them wondering what was bothering Molly. Pop started saying grace, "Dear Lord, we are thankful for our family, our crops, our home, and the food you provided for us today. We are thankful for the peacefulness You have given to us on this mountaintop, and for the sunshine and rain."

"Is he gonna thank the Lord for every thing we have in

this cabin?" Molly impatiently held her tongue.

"We are thankful for the love we share, and for our health." He looked up at Nina, "Do you have anything to add?"

"No, I think you've about covered it all."

"And for the new healthy calf." Pop paused again as Molly exhaled loudly. "Amen," he finally concluded.

Much to Molly's dismay, Pop continued talkin'. "I ran into the preacher today and asked him to stop over for supper next Sunday after church. Is that alright with ya, Nina?"

"Sure," she said favorably, "but you're gonna have to eat your fried chicken with a knife and fork."

"Alright," Pop conceded. "But, we don't need to put on airs for the preacher," Pop mumbled before taking a big bite of butter-covered corn.

"I think I'll bake an applesauce stack cake, too." Nina thought out loud.

"Sounds delicious," Pop declared, "we sure are livin' high on the hog. This supper is delicious." He took another bite of corn, before directing his attention toward Molly. "What did ya get into this afternoon?" He asked as he chomped the ear in a circular motion.

"I was out hunting for berries and met the neighbor boy," she pointed in the direction of the river, "down by the witness tree."

"One of the Moore *boys?*" Pop asked, as a sudden realization hit him like a blow to his gut. *"She's probably old enough to be going through the woman change,"* he gasped. A kernel of corn lodged in his windpipe. He started coughing and sputtering, as Nina slowly pushed back her chair and started pounding him hard on his back.

"It's okay, Pop. I'll have *the talk* with her soon," she whispered in his ear.

Still, his face dripped with concern. He began to breathe heavily as his nostrils flared like a tired horse, his mind racing, his blood pressure rising as he remembered back when he was a teenage boy.

"Yeah, the youngest of the Moore boys. His name is Zach." Molly chewed at her lip, trying to ignore Pop's panicked fit, all the time trying to get her nerve up to ask the big question. She chickened out. "We watched the clouds for a little while, and then…"

Nina interrupted her, "Did you see that big old warrior horse that was in the clouds today?"

"No, we saw a…"

Pop was profusely relieved the conversation had changed away from boys, and figured talkin' about anything else would help his heart quit fluttering. "I did see that warrior horse! I was puttin' out some salt licks and looked up and there it was, just as plain as could be. A big, mighty horse galloping across the sky."

Molly briefly measured how insignificant her sparrow was in comparison to a warrior horse, and started getting even madder. "Ya'll listen! This is important!" Molly chastised Nina and Pop.

They both stared at her wide-eyed, before Nina inquired, "Is there something botherin' ya, Molly?"

"As a matter-of-fact there is something botherin' me." She slammed her fork down on the table. "Are you my mama, Nina?"

"Of course, I'm your mama. What do ya mean?"

"Zach Moore asked me why I don't look like you or Pop. He said we weren't blood kin."

Nina and Pop studied one another, and for a long second, silence filled the room.

"That's just what I thought!" Molly angrily declared, "We're not blood, are we?"

Pop gently placed his fork to the side of his plate, "You don't need to have the same blood line to be a family, Molly. It don't matter where your roots start, not in America."

"So, we ain't blood?" Molly could feel the tears start to well up in her eyes.

"No, we ain't blood," Nina half whispered, "but we are family. Right, Pop?"

Pop could feel his own tears starting to cloud his vision. "Of course, we're family." His face tinged beet red. "Come here, Molly. Come here, Nina." He motioned for them to come close to him.

Nina and Molly slid back their chairs and Pop clutched them both, in a close fitting bear hug. The tears started streaming down his cheeks, as thankfulness soared from within. "I love both of you more than I have ever loved anyone in my life." He continued as he sobbed heavily, "We will always be family." He held on to them tight as his chest heaved up and down. "Out of all the folks in this big ole world, God blessed me." Pop squeezed them tighter. Pop Minion declared, once again disbelievingly, "And, God blessed me!" They could hear him murmur between hushed sobs, "We are the Minion clan."

This was all the reassurance Molly needed to hear, 'cause deep down in her heart, she knew it to be true.

Several moments had passed before Pop's breathing started to settle. Molly nudged his shoulder, "Pop?"

"Yes, Molly?" He sniffled.

"You're squashin' us."

Monongahela Mountains, West Virginia
May 29, 1916

Nina and Molly were just finishing up their early morning routine of milking cows when they overheard the scrunching sound of a person approaching from the West. Nina shouldered her rifle, directed Molly to stay inside the barn, and walked out to the pasture to see who was calling on them at such an early hour. Nina spied one of the Tucker boys, panting breathlessly, as he approached their cabin.

"We're over here!" Nina shouted to the youngster.

His attention turned toward her voice, and he began walking and talking so fast that Nina couldn't understand a word he was mumbling.

"Slow down a bit. Do you need a drink of water?"

He nodded his head slightly and Nina motioned for him to meet her by the well.

She handed him the ladle and he took a long gulp, followed by a deep breath, "Mama told me to come and fetch ya. Liza has been birthin' all night long and ain't nothin' comin' out. Mama's gettin' scared, she thinks the baby may be dead, and we ain't got no money to pay ya."

"You have some Ginseng don't ya?" Nina assured the child. "That will be all the pay I need." She could easily ascertain the boy was exhausted. "Did ya walk all the way over here from the holler?" Nina asked.

"Yep," the young boy panted, "I left out about three this mornin'."

"Let me hitch a horse to the wagon, and you can ride back with me and Molly." Her attention moved from the boy toward the barn, "Molly, run into the house and collect my satchel. You're going with me to Tucker Holler. I'm gonna need your help."

Molly ran into the house, snatched up Nina's medicine bag and was back out on the porch by the time the horse and wagon was ready to leave. Molly hopped up onto the wooden seat and slid in close to Nina, allowing room for the boy to be seated beside her. They rode in silence, down the mountain path to the road running beside the river, passing several farms along the way. Molly kept stealing glances at the Tucker boy, and consciously compared the color of her arm to his, as they bumped along the rocky path. *"You look more akin to the folks that live up Tucker Holler,"* she thought about Zach Moore's previous observation.

When they arrived at Tucker Holler, Molly was shocked to see the shacks lined up on the hillside. She curiously observed the large slits in the walls of the shacks and the folks who were sitting outside on the steps, as the wagon slowly rolled through the thick red clay sludge on the road. The boy pointed to a specific house, so Nina pulled the wagon along side a crabapple tree, snatched up her satchel, and hopped off the platform. Molly followed closely behind. Nina and Molly could see several men seated outside, their faces sodden with worry, and she could hear continuous cries resonating from within the modest wooden cabin.

"Thank ya for comin' so quickly, Ms. Nina." An older man, with an untrimmed black beard, acknowledged as he held the door open for them to enter. When they crossed over the doorsill, Molly was smacked in the face with intense heat, and she noticed flies swarming about everywhere, along with a penetrating odor she could not quite identify.

The young woman on the soiled mattress moaned again, her cries weaker now and gruff from the screaming that had been reverberating from within the small hut, probably long before they had first pulled up outside. The feather stuffed mattress, positioned in the corner of the one room shack, was soaked from the sweat that poured from her body, causing a sour smell to drift around the room. The windows were opened, but there was not enough of a breeze stirring about to cool her down.

Nina's face dropped with uneasiness as she looked down at the expectant mother. She dipped a clean rag into a bowl of lukewarm water and wiped the young woman's forehead, trying to give her the only comfort she could. The girl was barely fifteen, and so thin she could have been mistaken for a boy except for her swollen abdomen. Liza's eyes flickered open, landing on Nina's face in a quiet appeal. Since she had no reassurance to offer, she motioned for Molly to go fetch some more hot water.

When Molly returned she placed the bowl of water on the wood box situated by a window, and walked over to the corner where Nina was rubbing her hands over the pregnant girl's stomach. "The baby has been trying to come out feet-first, and it's a large child, too. I guess I'm gonna have to move the baby, but it is dangerous and painful." Nina glanced over her shoulder toward the older woman, who had been wordlessly sitting beside the bed. "I can't tell for sure if the child is still breathing, either."

"That's what I've been thinking, too. I've been prayin' for the baby but I don't think it's gonna help." The older woman dolefully fessed up, "The little one has been fightin' its way out for a long time. Maybe too long."

"Liza," Nina whispered, "this is gonna hurt something awful."

"Just help us," the young girl pleaded.

Molly watched in horror and astonishment, as Nina confidently reached up between the young woman's legs. Nina seemed to be able to ignore the screams of the mother, but Molly felt like crying. She didn't utter a word or allow any expression to cross her face. She just stared in empathy and compassion at the poor girl. There was blood trickling onto the mattress and flies were crawling everywhere. For a second, Molly felt sour bitterness rise into her throat. She swallowed deeply and fought back the urge to vomit. She didn't want to disappoint Nina, or make the Tucker folks think she was uppity. At this very moment though, she wished she were at home milking the cows.

Nina momentarily considered having one of the men or boys waiting outside go fetch Dr. Johnson, then remembered he only doctored white folks. She forcibly grasped the infant's feet and pulled down hard, as Liza let out an excruciating scream.

Molly passed out cold.

The next thing she remembered was opening her eyes, only to see the young boy, who had come to fetch them earlier, dabbing a wet cloth on her face. She popped straight up and looked toward the bed where she saw the girl curled up in a tight ball. The young, childless mother was sobbing now, and Nina was respectfully draping the motionless baby up in close-fitting layers of cotton cloth as the elderly woman uttered the Lord's Prayer.

The baby was a boy. A perfectly shaped, normal-looking

little boy, except his skin was tinged gray. He reminded Molly of a porcelain doll, still and frozen.

"You should hold the baby," Nina suggested to Liza, "it makes the grieving easier."

Liza took the woman's advice and held the little boy for a long while. She touched his hair gently, and rubbed her finger across his nose and cheeks. She handed the child to Nina, "Would you like to hold him for a minute?"

Nina bent over and gently lifted the little one from his mother's arms, "I would love to hold this darling child. Thank you, Liza, for offering." Nina stared at the child wondering exactly what had gone wrong. *"Did they wait too long to fetch help? How could the death of this child be a part of God's plan?"* Nina shook the thoughts from her mind as she placed the dead child beside the young girl.

"I guess we should be leaving you folks so you can mourn in your own way. I'm sorry." Nina motioned for Molly to join her and the elderly woman handed a poke full of Ginseng roots to Nina.

"No," Nina pushed them back to her. "I wasn't any help."

"'Tain't your fault." The woman replied. "Please take 'em. We always pay our debts."

Nina graciously accepted the offering, as she handed over a pouch filled with a medicinal elixir. "It's a sedative," she explained, "this tincture will give her four days of sweet dreams." She nodded her head toward the young woman curled up in the bed, "And she's gonna need them."

The older woman tilted her head cordially, "Thank you for comin' Ms. Nina."

"I will always come when ya need me," she guaranteed.

The moment Nina and Molly hopped back into the wagon, Molly shyly apologized, "I'm so sorry 'bout what happened in there."

"Don't you worry child, I've seen many a strong man have the same reaction." Nina teased, "Only they hit the floor a lot harder than you did."

Nina clicked her tongue to get the horses rolling.

"Will the little baby go straight to heaven?" The young girl whispered as she thought back over it all.

"Absolutely." Nina promised, "God is merciful and loves little children." She took in a deep breath, "You also have to understand that birthin' isn't always as hard as what you saw in there, sometimes it goes as smooth as corn silk."

Molly pondered on all she had witnessed for a few moments, before she blurted straight-out, "Where did I come from Nina?" She was supposing, "Was it Tucker Holler?"

"No, Molly." Nina reassured, "You were a gift from God." She offered up a downhearted smile, "Why do you care where you came from, anyway? All that matters is where you're going." She squinted at the young woman as she gauged her reaction, "Right?"

"I reckon," Molly conceded as her eyes misted with fresh tears. She had noticed that the tint of her skin was lighter than the folks in the holler, and her hair wasn't nearly as dark, or as tightly curled either. *"But my eyes are the same color,"* she imagined.

They rode in silence until they had left the earshot of the humble folks in the holler and turned onto a narrow mountain path. "Molly," Nina approached in a serious tone of voice, "there is something I need to explain to you."

It was during this gloomy ride home from Tucker Holler that Molly learned, in excruciating detail, about the birds and the bees, the horses and the sow, and Nina even told her a pointed story about free milk and a cow.

It was a day's worth of lessons Molly was quite sure she would never forget.

Springfield Senior Care Facility
1990
"Shy of a Quart"

"Lord have mercy," Allison declared. "Birthin' ain't easy." She leaned over, hiked up her skirt a couple inches, and withdrew a hand-rolled cigarette from her knee-high hose. "Smoke?"

"No, thank you. I never quite had the notion to try one." Molly responded as she scanned the veranda searching for a container for the imposing woman to use as a snuff for her cigarette when she was finished. *"This is a non-smoking facility,"* Molly carefully considered the regulations set forth in her occupancy agreement.

"I will tell you this," Allison confessed as she struck a match, "I wish I would have witnessed the Tucker birth. Had I done so, I might not have ended up unwed and pregnant at the age of sixteen." Allison inhaled deeply. "My life could have ended up a lot better." She shrugged her shoulders, "Or maybe not. Who knows?"

Molly pushed an empty flowerpot beside Allison's drink to serve as an ashtray. "It made an impression on me," she admitted, "that's for sure."

"Did you accompany Nina on many of her calls?"

"Quite a few," she reflected, "but none stuck in my mind like the Tucker Holler birthing."

"Did you ever consider being a midwife? A lot of folks carry on in the family business. I think it's because the family business is all they have been exposed to, but it may have to do with learning a craft at an early age." Allison slanted her head to the side and blew rings of smoke into the air.

"I didn't take up being a midwife, but I..."

Allison cut in on Molly's response, "My family didn't have much of a trade to learn, so my only choice in life was to get married or to get married," she released a shrilling cackle. "The first fellow I married was the biggest mistake I made in my life. He was one of those men who were always tryin' to make their girl jealous. You know the type. He had low self-esteem so he figured he'd make me love him more with his diminutive games. Being married to him was like havin' a raspberry seed stuck between my teeth." She picked at her tooth for emphasis. "I put him out on the porch, as Grandma Thorne used to say, and locked the back door."

"Well, at least you were smart enough to know when to fold 'em." Molly cleverly interjected lyrics from a Kenny Rogers song.

"That's for sure." Allison offered an earnest look. "Heck, I didn't learn to read until I was twenty years old." She waggled her finger in Molly's direction, "But once I did learn, I devoured books like they were chocolate. Ernest Hemingway was my favorite. But, of course, Tennessee Williams could paint a vivid tale and John Steinbeck," she proliferated with a wink, "was just downright scandalous."

"You are a literary lion, Allison." Molly sincerely observed.

Allison held her cigarette up with two fingers, "Give this a try, Molly. I roll them myself."

A resonant smile enveloped Molly's cheeks as she thought of Nina and Pop lounging on the porch smoking the distinctive tobacco that Nina grew out between the rows of corn at the edge of the field. She would dry it out, upside-down, in the smokehouse, dabble it, almost to the top, into a quart-size cobalt jar, tap one singular hole in the lid, and label the top with a rudimentary scratch of a nail, indicating the date of harvest.

"Close your eyes, Pop." Nina would say, *"What can you smell?"*

"Soil, and the barn." He chuckled.

"What can you hear?"

"The pigs squealing – they sound like children." He offered up.

"Tell me something you'll always remember feeling." She probed.

"Being tucked in close to you." He teased.

"Pop, you're ornery. Molly is sitting right here."

A chuckle escaped from deep in his belly. *"Okay. The rough, hairy skin of a sow's back."*

Molly remembered the entire conversation, as if it was a movie reel running in her mind. Nina, Pop, and little Molly would play this game over and over again as they watched the sun brighten from the yellow hue of a Black-eyed Susan to the deep pink of a Red Clover, right before it tucked itself in behind the mountain for the night.

"Give it a try?" Allison offered again.

"No, thanks anyway."

Allison inhaled deeply, and the smoke felt like fire scouring her lungs as she began coughing and hacking incessantly.

Molly studied her carefully, half wondering if they were going to have to make a quick trip to the emergency room. When she spied a young woman walking along the path, only a few feet away, she frantically directed Allison's attention toward the interloper.

"Oh, Lordy." Allison mumbled as she dropped the cigarette into the flowerpot, "The steely, unyielding Nurse Ratched."

Molly started laughing, and Allison joined in, between the hacks and coughs, as tears copiously cascaded down her cheeks.

They didn't realize I had overheard the derogatory slam, nor did they realize, at this point in the story, that I would be writing about their adventures.

"What are you ladies up to?" I inquired with an exaggerated arch of my brow. "Allison," I pointedly glared, "you surely aren't over here corrupting Molly. Are you?"

Allison let out a loud energetic chuckle and smacked her knee enthusiastically. "I'm trying, Carolyn," she winked at me. "But she ain't cooperating."

I pinched my lips together in a line, as I tried not to laugh and jiggled my finger at them both, "You two best stay out of trouble." I kept walking up the path, but not before turning around to warn them, "I've got my eyes on you two!"

Allison poked her tongue out, and they burst into a fit of hilarity. I sarcastically mumbled, loud enough for them to overhear, "This older generation is going to be the ruin of us all." I turned the corner, leaving them giggling like they were three pickles shy of a quart.

Monongahela Mountains, West Virginia
July 3, 1916

Zach was leaning up against the witness tree, twisting a wire on the end of his fishing pole, when he heard Molly's feet crunching through the bush.

"What took ya so long, Molly? I've been waitin' here for a coon's age."

Molly propped her hand on her hip, "Sorry. Nina had me hanging the clean clothes on the line and she suddenly decided to wash up all the bed linens." She exhaled exasperatedly, "I couldn't believe she picked today to wash up the sheets."

"It's okay. Are ya ready to go fishin'? I brought some worms and an extra pole. Do you know how to bait a hook?"

Molly looked at him as if he had lost his mind, "Do I know how to bait a hook? You're as silly as a goose, Zach Moore, of course I know how to bait a hook. I've been fishing since before you were born."

"So you ain't afraid to put on the worm?" He teased.

"Give me that worm, I'll show ya how to double it up on there." She pointed toward his pole.

Zach took off running down toward the river, "Last one to the stream is a rotten egg!"

"Not fair! You got a head start," Molly yelled out, as she followed behind him.

They found a big flat rock to sit on and patiently cast their lines. There were fish in the river, big, swift, beautiful fast-water fish. They weren't like catfish, lying lazily on the shallow bottom, they were darters, seen in a flash and then gone.

Molly yanked on the fishing line, "Missed him." Her eyes grew wide, "Did you see that big ole crappie?"

The corner of Zach's mouth was twitching, and Molly had the distinct feeling he was trying not to laugh, "That wasn't no crappie, it was a trout."

"Look Zach, I don't want to be contrary. If you tell me that fish was a trout, even though I know good and well it's a crappie, that's fine with me." She rolled her eyes, "I might be a girl, but I've helped Pop wash the horses since I was a pony myself, and I know a crappie when I see one."

Zach considered this carefully as a stone expression covered his face. "Do you mean *warsh* the horses?" Zach was smiling now, his chiseled features altered from rigid angles and planes, to crinkles at the corners of his eyes, and she noticed the distinct hollow of a dimple highlighted one cheek.

"No, I don't mean *warsh*, I mean *wash*. The word *wash* ain't got the letter 'r' in it."

Zach scrunched his nose up, "It don't matter if it has an 'r' in it or not. Ya still say warsh."

Molly released a loud sigh, as she studied his features, "How come you only got one dimple?"

He lifted his hand to trace the dent in his face. "I was swinging on a grapevine and when it broke I thumped down onto the ground. Plop! A stick jabbed straight through my cheek. I could feel the wood branch inside of my mouth with my tongue."

"We'll I'll be." Molly ran her finger over her own cheek. "That must have been a smart painful, wasn't it?"

"Heck yeah. It hurt like the dickens when mama pulled it out, too."

"I bet," Molly figured.

"And when she poured the salt in it, I nearly passed out cold on the floor." Zach admitted.

Just then, Molly felt a fish tug at her line and rapidly jerked to secure the hook.

"Dawg-gone-it, Molly. Don't yank so hard," Zach advised, "you'll rip his lip off."

She slowly pulled the fish towards her. "Got one comin' in, Zach." She whispered. She carefully towed the line closer and closer, slowly, careful to not reel it in too fast. When it was near enough for her to grab, she reached into the cold stream and wrapped her hand around it, pushing down, away from its eyes so she could keep the gills flat while she expertly extracted the hook from its mouth. She held it up high for Zach to see, "What do ya think about this, Zach Moore?"

"Beginner's luck," he concluded.

"Beginner's luck?" Her jaw dropped open, "Well, I oughta whack this fish right over your head."

Zach let out a loud, heartfelt laugh and Molly started giggling along with him. The two friends tossed the fish into a bucket of water before casting their lines again. They sat in comfortable silence for hours, watching the fish dart, dipping their toes in the cool rushing water, snacking on walnuts and boiled eggs, and listening for the swooshing sound of flying squirrels, dashing like an arrow, from tree to tree.

"Life don't get no better than this," Zach declared as he nudged Molly.

"Amen," Molly pinched him on the side, and he jumped when her fingers found a ticklish spot. "Thanks for being my friend, Zach Moore."

He rustled his foot through the stream, splashing her with water, and his gaze turned away, "I reckon I love you, Molly Minion."

Monongahela Mountains, West Virginia
July 19, 1916

The overcast sky that afternoon was swept a shimmering blue by a northerly breeze by the time Molly made it to the witness tree.

"Molly?" Zach whispered, "Look there." He pointed at two squirrels that were majestically gliding through the treetops.

"They are beautiful," Molly acknowledged as the last rags of the sun-washed clouds disappeared down the valley. "Nina says there is a hidden spirit of the wilderness, she says it's full of mystery, melancholy and charm. Those amazing squirrels are a perfect example of the secrets here in these mountains." Molly noticed the cliff faces a mile away showed their flinty details as if they were close enough to touch.

"I heard there was a whole bunch of 'em over on Seneca Rock. I'd like to go there someday. Do ya want to go with me?"

"Sure," Molly shrugged, "why not?"

"Let's plan on it," Zach suggested, "we could borrow a horse and take a picnic basket all the way to the top." A dreamy look covered their faces as they cast their eyes over the bright green stretches of foliage.

The squirrels had raised their heads and were looking down at them. They had heard the voices. They were alert, beautiful, and tiny at this distance, the enormous dark mountainside rising a thousand feet into the clouds behind them.

Suddenly they heard a man's voice bellow. "What are ya doin' down here with that nasty girl?"

"Nothin'," Zach startled as he jumped to his feet, "we're just watching the squirrels fly."

"Are you back-talkin' me?"

"No, Sir."

"You shouldn't be socializin' with them type of folks. Her mama is a heathen Injun, and," he spat dark liquid on the ground, "if you ain't noticed, that girl is an illiterate half-breed." He pointed his finger toward Molly. "Ya don't need to be mixin' with her kind."

Molly was afraid to take her eyes off the lumbering man. *"Half-breed? Injun? What in the tarnation is he talkin' about?"* Molly had never heard those words, but she could tell by the way they rolled off the mean man's tongue, he didn't mean nothin' good by them. Anger lifted off the large man like a bad smell. *"Why would he think I'm illiterate?"* She rose to her feet.

"She ain't a half-breed," Zach squared his shoulders, "she's my friend."

"I'll beat you to death, you stupid kid. Don't you *ever* talk back to me." The rage mirrored on Mr. Moore's face, as he unhitched the belt from around his waistband and wrapped the leather around his hand. The angry man drew the boy toward him by the hair on his head, and soon the cries of the young boy, and the sound of a snapping whip, echoed up the mountain.

"Mister," Molly screamed, "quit hitting him!" Her heartbeat was skipping and fluttering. The man's eyes were terrible, burning with naked hate.

He stared at Molly with those malevolent, black eyes. "Get your ass up the mountain! Or I'll beat you, too."

Molly looked at Zach who was heaped over on the ground, trying to protect himself from the belt that kept thrashing him on his arms and face. For a brief second, she recognized embarrassment, or more likely shame, covering his face. She took off, running up the mountain. Her chest was heaving, and she kept trying to scream for Nina, but the fear and sobs veiled her voice.

She kept stumbling up toward the cabin, ignoring the briars that were scratching at her legs. Her mind felt disoriented, ashamed, confused. She fell once and could feel a sharp rock stab into her knee, causing blood to begin streaming down her leg. She stood up and looked around. For a brief moment, she was so muddled she didn't know where she was standing, or which way she needed to run. *"Up, up, the mountain,"* she gazed at the treetops. When she reached the high ground where the hill sloped off toward the river, she glanced back at the boulders by the edge of the creek, watching to see if Mr. Moore had followed her. By the time she saw her cabin, the salt of tears had scoured her vision. She fell to her knees as her chest throbbed.

Nina had seen her approaching, through a slit in the wood of the chicken coop, and she hastily discarded the eggs to her side. She rushed to meet her. "What's wrong, Molly? Did somebody hurt ya?"

Molly shook her head no. Nina touched the child's face to pull back a rope of wet hair that hung over her eye. Molly tried to speak but the words would not escape from her throat.

Nina rushed to the well and pulled up a bucket of water, scooped the ladle full, and handed it to her daughter. "Take a drink, Molly. Try to calm down. I need to know what has happened." She snatched up a dirty rag lying by the well and poured water on it, twisted it to wring the water out and gently placed it on Molly's bleeding knee.

Between uncontrollable gasps, Molly said, "Mr. Moore was beating Zach. It was awful! He called us half-breeds, and Injun's, he said I was illiterate, and I was afraid." She desperately stared into Nina's eyes, "And I left Zach." She shook her head "I left him alone, just left him there, while his daddy beat him!" She started crying all over again, "I didn't even try to help him, Nina."

"Half-breed? Injun?" Nina fumed. *"Illiterate? Did that stupid drunk mean illegitimate?"* She shook her head in astonishment. Nina spent a great deal of time teaching Molly how to read and write, and she thanked God that while Molly knew the difference between illiterate and illegitimate, Frank Moore did not. "It's okay, Molly. You did the right thing." She helped the young girl up, "I assure you can read better than any one of the Moore clan." Frank Moore's narrow-mindedness infuriated her. "Come into the cabin and try to quit crying." She hugged Molly tight and shepherded her through the cabin door. "Don't pay no mind to Mr. Moore. He's so stupid he couldn't pour rain out of a boot if the directions were written on the heel."

Molly curiously stared at Nina.

"He is absolutely as useless as a tit on a boar hog," she muttered.

Nina's fury somehow comforted Molly, and although it took several long moments to calm her down, the child was eventually able to quit sobbing.

Nina snapped a leaf of Blackwort and smeared it over the cuts, before wrapping a clean cloth around the child's leg. She immediately snatched up a long rifle, which lay across its two pegs on the far wall, and the bullet bag hanging underneath it, before directing Molly to stay inside. "I'll be back in a few minutes, Molly. Don't let anyone in the door and don't go outside. Pop should be coming home shortly."

"Where are you headed, Nina?" Molly asked with concern.

"Gonna call on Frank Moore," she glanced at Molly who still had salty tear streams caking her face, "and don't tell Pop. Okay?"

"Why are you taking the gun?" Molly gulped, "You're not going to shoot him, are ya?"

"I ain't plannin' on it." She pursed her lips together with determination, "But I ain't dismissin' the prospect."

Nina took off walking through the woods, her feet scrunching through the undergrowth, her every movement causing the thicket to snap and rustle. She wanted Frank to know she was coming, so she intentionally took heavy steps while clearing the forest weeds out of her way with the butt of her rifle. She hoped the spineless drunk was shaking in his boots as he heard her approach. *"I'm gettin' feelings I needn't,"* she supposed. *"But, I can't quite help it,"* she trudged along hastily. *"Did he call my Molly a half-breed?"* Her mind was racing.

By the time she arrived at the Moore's cabin, she was as riled up as a hornet's nest that had been poked with a stick. When she didn't see anyone outside, she climbed the few steps and rapped three sturdy times on the wooden door, before wiping the sweat from her brow.

"Come on in," she heard a man's voice, "it's open."

Nina pushed the door open and stepped over the threshold into the one room home of the Moore family.

Everyone who lived on the mountaintop knew Nina most always carried her rifle with her, so there would be no need for concern. She nonchalantly tucked the gun under her arm, barrel end pointing toward the floor, and scanned the folks who were gathered around the table. She could discern Frank had been drinking when she spied the redness encircling his eyelids. His youngest son bore injuries from the recent beating that covered every inch of his face, arms and upper body. The boy's mother was applying a wet cloth to the wounds, and her gaze dropped to the floor when Nina attempted to make eye contact. Yeah, that's what she thought. Nina knew what was going on here, she had seen it over and over again during her lifetime, and she didn't like it. Not one little bit. Frank was a big, strong man who apparently liked to hit around on those who were smaller and weaker. *"Coward,"* Nina thought disgustedly.

"Frank," Nina directed her attention toward the revolting man, "I heard you were using some mighty distasteful language around my Molly."

Frank smirked, causing Nina's stare to sharpen.

"I don't rightly care much for the dirty words you were using around my child." Nina arched her eyebrow, "And my girl knows how to read, if that's what you were implying – when you called her illiterate."

"What? I never said she couldn't read, I said she was…was…ill…ill…"

Nina interrupted the blabbering idiot. "To tell ya the truth, I don't care much for you slapping around on your family. Where I come from, a man who strikes his family is thought of as a pathetic lily liver."

"Where exactly is it you come from, Nina?" He sneered,

briefly waiting for her response. "This here ain't none of your business. It's my family and ya don't need to be sticking your nose into other folks manure." He spat the words out.

"Well, Frank." Nina paused as she bit at her lower lip, "Manure, it surely is, and you made it my business when you voiced your distasteful accusations." She pointedly stared at the man. "Why don't we talk this over out on the porch?" She suggested, adding a slight tilt of her head.

"Sure," he sarcastically mumbled as he suddenly rose out of his chair, causing it to tumble to the floor.

When Nina stepped onto the porch she secured her rifle with both hands. Frank stumbled out and closed the door behind him, sliding a pinch of snuff under his lip.

"Nina," he narrowed his brow, "we're selling our land to the government and gonna be moving off this mountain in just a couple of weeks. So, I would suggest you just get your little red ass over there on your property before one of us gets hurt."

Nina stared at him long and hard before replying, "I figure you're right. No reason to cause any trouble." She turned to walk off the porch, and strategically slung her rifle over her shoulder, deliberately smacking Frank square in the nose with the wooden gunstock.

"Damn woman!" He screamed out, as his hands rose to cover his face, "You done broke my nose!"

She twisted around to face him, "Oh, I do apologize for my clumsiness." Nina replied, most insincerely.

"You hit me on purpose! I oughta beat you to death," he furiously murmured through clenched teeth.

She noticed blood and snuff streaming through his fingers, down his chin and dripping onto his shirt. "Frank

Moore," her eyes narrowed to tiny slits as she swung her weapon around and positioned the metal stock in the direction of his oversized gut, "you're lucky I don't scalp the last three hairs off your ugly bald head and prop your hide on a post. After all, I am an Injun, ya know."

Nina flashed a sarcastic smile toward him, before she took off casually strolling down the porch steps. She cocked the rifle loudly, holding it high above her head for him to see. She sauntered across the isolated mountain toward her own land, and didn't bother to look back.

Later the same evening, when Pop Minion came home, Nina and Molly had supper ready and placed it on the table after Pop had washed up. Molly said grace, and they began feasting on biscuits, potatoes, onions, and deer tenderloin that had been simmering all day.

Pop Minion ate a few bites before announcing to the family, "I stopped over at Frank Moore's house on my way home this evening." He slopped up the gravy on the side of his dish before he polished off his last bite of biscuit. "I talked to his oldest son and he said his family was selling out and moving to Pittsburgh."

"Is that right?"

"Yeah," Pop nodded his head. "He also said Frank took a nasty tumble down the steps of his own front porch." Pop peeped at Nina.

She studiously avoided eye contact.

"He broke his nose. It's flatter than a pancake. His son said he figured it will be hurtin' for a long spell."

"Well, I'll be." Nina shoved a bite of the tender meat into her mouth and began to slowly chew.

Molly's eyes grew wide as she stared, startled, at Nina.

"Yep, he said it was right after you visited the family this afternoon." Pop smashed at a potato with his fork. "You didn't see him take a tumble down the steps. Did ya, Nina?"

"I did not witness Frank fallin' down no steps," Nina honestly declared.

Pop seemed to consider her statement carefully. He suddenly stopped chewing and looked at Nina, toward Molly, and back at Nina again. He swallowed deeply. "You know, Jesus says to love thy neighbor," he took a long gulp of milk before continuing, "and the New Testament teaches us to forgive one another."

Nina gently placed her fork down on the wooden table beside her plate. "Ya know, Pop," she crossed her hands under her chin and looked him straight in the eye, "I'm still tryin' to digest the Old Testament. I ain't quite got around to the New Testament, yet."

"Yeah," he dipped his head slowly and thoughtfully, "there's a lot to take in. It's a big book." He winked at Nina, "Could ya pass me another biscuit, please?"

A few days after Frank Moore fell down his front steps and broke his nose, his wife showed up outside the smokehouse, where Nina and Molly were tying Lavender into bunches before hanging them upside down in the eaves for drying.

"Ms. Nina," Frank's wife said as she stared at a distant tree, "I know you don't much care for my husband," her gaze fell to the ground, "but, he's been havin' difficulties in the outhouse."

"Difficulties?" Nina's eyes sparked as delight trickled down her spine. "Is the problem liquid or solid?"

Mrs. Moore cyphered for a flash before replying, "It should be a solid, but now it's a liquid, I reckon ya could say."

"Is that right?" Nina placed her finger on her chin as if she was carefully considering the situation. "I know just what to give him," she wagged her finger in assurance, "White Bryony." She strolled into the house and snatched up a strong laxative, poured it into a tiny bottle, and returned to the front yard. "Add a few drops to his tea three times a day for a week," she said as she handed the tincture to the other woman.

"Thank ya, kindly." Mrs. Moore said as she accepted the mixture.

"My pleasure," Nina replied, as the corner of her mouth twinged.

Pop, who had overheard the entire conversation, was so confused that he didn't know whether to scratch his pocket watch or wind his butt. He slowly moseyed over to Nina, who was surveying Frank's wife cut through the bushy path adjoining their properties. "I know I ain't an expert on herbs like you are," he speculated curiously, "but ain't that gonna make his condition worse?"

"It surely is," Nina clapped her hands together joyfully, "it surely is."

Pop swatted her behind affectionately. "Woman, you are downright ornery."

Springfield Senior Care Facility
1990
"Misadventures"

"Goodness gracious," Allison declared. "I guess Frank Moore got what he deserved." She propped her elbows on the table and plunked her chin into her hands, "Did you ever see Zach again?"

"No. I never went back to the witness tree," Molly sadly admitted. "However, every single time I see the clouds forming shapes in the sky, I fondly remember Zach Moore."

Allison leaned over and gave her friend's shoulder a quick pat, "I'm sorry."

"It was just one of those things," she hopelessly threw her hand in the air.

"We're both sittin' in amen corner," Allison confessed. "One can never tell why life takes the turns it does." Her eyes widened as she suggested, "You should have someone write your memoir. Nurse Ratched is majoring in journalism." Allison confided, "She's not really a nurse. She just helps out around here, and we should ask her to join us. You really have experienced quite a remarkable life, you know it, Molly?"

"Not really," Molly replied. "But, it is fun to reminisce."

"Do you know what is fun for me? Sketching. I'm not good. I just enjoy it."

"That does sound like a fun hobby, Allison."

"Be right back," Allison quickly stood up. "Whoa," she stumbled, "I think my knee may have went out." She gyrated her leg for several long seconds attempting to work the kink out.

Molly laughed as she stood and informed Allison that she needed to do a few chores, and suggested they meet on the patio later in the evening. Several hours later, after Molly had changed the sheets on her bed, successfully completed four small loads of laundry and devoured a peanut butter and jelly sandwich, she stepped from the living room into the kitchen only to realize her sliding-glass door was open. Molly gasped in horror. *"Where is Woody?"* She frantically moved from room to room calling for her tabby cat. The last time she had seen him he was rolling around in catnip in a patch of sunlight on the kitchen rug. "Woody?" She called as she turned her ear up to listen. He always responded when Molly called his name, so she was sure he had escaped through the door that was left ajar.

"Allison," Molly yelled out, "are you out there?" She peeped through the window to see her next-door neighbor scribbling in a notebook on the veranda. Her hair was now tightly wound around pink perm curlers.

"Yep," she hollered back, "I'm right here."

"Have you seen Woody?"

"Who's Woody?"

"Woody is my cat!" Molly perched her hand on her hip, "Have you seen him?"

Allison's face dripped apologetically. "I'm so sorry. He said he had to pee."

"Did you read the plaque beside the door?" Molly sarcastically inquired.

Allison gulped, "What plaque?"

"Come in here," she waggled her finger, "look!"

Allison followed Molly into the kitchen, squinted her eyes, and read the wooden hand-painted marker aloud.

"Don't let the cat out. No matter what he tells you!" She turned to face her friend, "I'm so sorry, Molly. I didn't pay attention."

"You're going to have to help me find him," Molly half barked.

"Of course, I'll help you. I'd help you find him even if it wasn't my fault." She patted Molly's arm sincerely, "Let me grab a couple of flashlights, because it's going to be getting dark soon."

Molly tossed off her flip-flops and slid into her reliable sneakers as she impatiently waited for Allison to return. She could feel her blood pressure rising throughout each waning moment, and she simply wanted to pinch Allison's head off. *"Snap! Just like a leaf of Blackwort!"* She imagined. *"I knew she was going to be nothing but trouble. Why did I ask her to join me for tea? I should have listened to my instincts."*

When Allison returned, after several very long moments, she was sporting pink curlers, rubber boots, and a purple-dotted housedress, all the time carrying two large flashlights.

"Let's go." She finally announced. "I think we should head in the direction of City Park. What do you think?"

"I think we better find him," Molly replied through clenched teeth. "Let's start with the complex first."

"Of course we will find him, Molly. Don't you worry."

They took off in the direction of the parking lot, yelling "Woody" every few minutes, and then pausing, to pin their ears back, listening for a response. They traipsed the entire L-shaped, forty double-story, cedar-shingled room facility twice with no luck. On their third attempt around the building, they snapped on the flashlights and started shouting "Woody" every few seconds.

"Woody?"

"Woody!"

"WOODY!" Molly's voice grew louder and more desperate with each beckoning call.

"I got a woody up here for you, Allison." They heard a man's voice yell out from the second floor balcony.

Allison shone her light in his direction, only to witness an elderly man making revolting thrusting motions with his hips.

"You are disgusting Mr. Farmer." Allison hollered at him. "I have curlers in my hair! Goodness gracious!"

He released a muted chuckle.

"That man is a pervert," Allison said. "He is like a hundred years old and all he thinks about is sex. He grabbed my butt while I was in the elevator last week."

Molly gasped in disbelief.

Allison paused and glimpsed at Molly. "I wonder if he's eligible?" She asked with interest.

Molly shuddered when she considered Allison's indiscriminating taste in men, and grabbed ahold of her arm to steer her away. "Let's check out City Park. Woody is obviously not around here."

They climbed the hill and started making their way along the path that led to the park benches, scanning every inch of the ground with their lights as they trudged along. Allison suddenly held up her hand indicating they should halt. She shone her light in the direction of some thick bushes and whispered, "I hear something over there. Maybe it's Woody." She made a motion with her hand for Molly to follow her so they tiptoed over to the location where the shrubs were rustling. Molly slowly took her free hand and parted the thick greenery. Allison pointed her beaming light toward the noise, and they both jumped backward when they caught sight of a large, bare rump. There, much to their surprise, was a young, buck-naked, couple.

"Hey!" The young man indignantly declared. "What are you doing?"

"Sorry," Allison said. "We are looking for a lost cat."

"Obviously, we haven't seen any cats around here, Lady." The young man pointedly glared into the bright light.

"No," the woman confirmed his statement, "no cats."

"We are so sorry," Molly murmured as she pulled at Allison's arm.

"We apologize for the interruption," Allison declared, "carry on."

"Highly unlikely," they could hear the young man mumble as they turned away and headed further down the path.

When they were out of earshot Allison whispered in bogus disgust, "Well, I never!" She glanced toward Molly. "Okay, actually I have," she confessed. "It was quite a long time ago." She giggled, "So long ago, I can't remember all the details."

"No need to share."

"I don't mind to share," Allison offered, "if you're ever interested."

Molly held her hand up to pause Allison, "Not right now. Thanks anyway."

So, they picked along for over an hour shouting, "Woody," with no response. Molly was getting discouraged, and when they observed a sheriff's car pull up alongside of them, she went into a full-blown state of panic. "Allison, he's gonna know you have been smoking, and I'm going to be tossed out of my apartment for violating my lease agreement. I knew I shouldn't have let you smoke your cigarette on my patio. For goodness sake! We live in a strict non-smoking facility. Or worse, we're going to jail for trespassing on city property after hours!"

Allison jumped behind Molly, "Maybe we should make a break for it," she suggested.

Molly nodded in agreement and they took off running – actually it was more of a brisk walk – in the direction of the senior care facility.

"Hold up!" They could hear the officer shout, "What are you ladies doing here in the park so late at night?"

They sped their pace.

"Freeze!" The young sheriff bellowed.

They halted before turning around to face him.

He sauntered over to the women and articulately enunciated, "What are you doing here at this late hour? It's not safe to be in the park after dark."

"We are looking for a lost cat," Allison informed him. "Maybe you can help us."

The sheriff eyed them suspiciously. "Do you ladies belong at the senior care facility?"

Molly puffed up, immediately recognizing that the young officer was presuming they were old and senile. "Humph!" she snorted loudly. "What would ever give you that impression?"

"Neither of you are carrying a pocketbook or car keys," he pointedly glared at Allison's pink curlers, "and the senior care facility is the only building within walking distance." His gaze narrowed.

"Oh." Molly smiled at him. "You are very observant,

Officer."

"Hop in the cruiser and I'll give you a ride home." He motioned for them to follow him.

Allison and Molly slid into the back seat. As he made the sharp right turn into the parking lot, Allison requested he turn on the blue flashing lights. "It will give the neighbors something to talk about," she cackled devilishly.

The officer flipped on the lights and added a complimentary blast of his siren, as he pulled up along side the community room, popped open the front door and politely opened the back door of the cruiser for them. When they were safely planted on the sidewalk, he loudly declared, "You two best stay out of trouble." He provided a teasing wink before authoritatively barking, "I don't want to see either one of you again."

Allison tittered with delight as several residents, including Mr. Farmer, the so-called pervert, and various staff members, inquisitively stared from the balcony.

"Allison," Molly reminded her as they snuck around the corner, "we still didn't locate Woody. I am not quitting until he is found."

"Let's take another jaunt around the grounds," Allison shot her a pleading glance, "if it's alright with you, I need to stop and use the potty."

"A quick potty break," Molly conceded.

They trotted to Molly's apartment, where she slid the key into the lock, and flicked on the lights, only to spy Woody, curled up in a tight ball, sleeping peacefully on the sofa. "Would ya look there, Allison? He has been right here all evening."

"That's just like a male for you," Allison replied as she hurried toward the bathroom. "Getting us all riled up over nothing."

Allison left the bathroom door open and Molly could overhear her tinkling from the living room.

"Molly?" Allison yelled out as she flushed the toilet. "I have a rectal exam in the morning. Would you like to accompany me to the doctor's office?"

"Why would I attend your rectal exam?"

"It would be fun."

"Fun?" Molly rolled her eyes dramatically. "I don't think so. I'm going be really busy in the morning. Mm-hmm. Very busy."

Allison shuffled into the living room, "Busy doing what?"

A flood of random excuses rushed through her head, but she couldn't think of one solitary response.

Allison wiggled her finger in the air, "Just as I thought. Be ready at nine o'clock. Nurse Ratched is driving me, so we can ask her about writing your memoir." She stretched down and rubbed Woody's head. "See you bright and early."

The following morning, I pulled my silver Nissan along side the community room and patiently waited for Allison. Her appointment wasn't for over an hour, but I had firsthand experience in chauffeuring Allison, and knew there would be several stops involved in today's adventure. I must say I was a little shocked to see Molly saunter out the door with Allison in tow, but I figured, the more the merrier. I loved spending time with the older folks here at the care facility, and enjoyed hearing their stories and words of wisdom. Allison yanked open the back door of my Nissan and both women slid into the back seat.

"You don't mind if we ride back here, do you Carolyn?" Allison didn't wait for a response, "It will be like we are riding in the back of a limousine. Movie stars!" She held her hand up, anticipating a high-five.

Molly offered a clap of her hand in response.

I peeked through the rear view mirror before replying, "Just as long as the two of you can refrain from calling me Nurse Ratched." I added a playful arch of my brow.

"Ooops," Allison and Molly laughed, "you overheard us, eh?"

"Indeed, I did, and I was crushed." I held my hand over my heart, "Absolutely crushed."

Allison gasped sincerely, "I am so sorry, Carolyn. Really, I am. I didn't mean anything by the comment, I was just trying to be humorous."

"I'm kidding you," I taunted, "but I just got your goat, didn't I?"

Allison released a sarcastic, "Humph," as I punched on the gas. "Off to the proctologist!" I teased, "Good times!"

After we had made the sharp turn to exit the parking lot, Allison tapped me on the shoulder and sheepishly inquired, "Do you mind stopping at the service station up here on the left? I need to pee."

"We just left the complex, Allison." I informed her.

"I know, I know," she shrugged her shoulders. "The truth is, there's a beefcake that works behind the counter at the gas station and I try to stop in to flirt with him every chance I get."

"Allison," I sighed, "the young man who works behind

the counter is about twelve years old. You'll end up getting arrested. Which reminds me, did I see the police dropping you off at the facility last night?"

Allison giggled, "Yes, Molly just about got us arrested." She carried on as I heard Molly groan melodramatically. "Anyway, the man at the service station is not twelve, he is eighteen. I asked the last time I stopped."

"Sure, he is." I begrudgingly steered my Nissan into the station's lot. "I'll just wait for you here."

Allison cracked open her door and asked Molly to accompany her. "You have to see this guy. He is cute."

A full ten minutes later, Allison and Molly returned to the car with a bag stuffed full of gum, candy, and Little Debbie snack cakes.

"Did you pee, Allison?" I asked.

"Yes, I did. Thank you so much for asking." She answered sarcastically.

"Did you steal a look at Mr. Beefcake?" I probed.

Allison nodded enthusiastically, "Yes, we did. He waited on us, actually. I was going to ask him for his phone number but Molly cut me off."

Molly piped in, "You were right about him, Allison. He is as fit as a butcher's dog. But, I do agree with Carolyn, I think he is too young for you."

"I have a young heart," Allison mumbled as she retrieved a pack of Juicy Fruit from her goody bag. She slid out a piece and handed one to Molly and dangled one over the front seat for me.

"Carolyn," Allison tapped me on the shoulder again, "I have been thinking about your writing career and feel as if you should write Molly's memoir. She has had the most interesting life of anyone I have ever met. The stories she has been telling me are simply…" she paused to find the right word, "remarkable."

"It really hasn't been that remarkable," Molly shyly interrupted.

"Are you kidding? Hangings, floods, and Indians. Who do you know that has better tales?" Allison continued, "Absolutely amazing!"

"Seriously?" My interest piqued. "I would love to hear your life story, for sure."

"Great," Allison slapped her knee, "settled." Her eyes wrinkled up as a smile spanned her face, "We'll start tomorrow."

The next morning I arrived early, equipped with my cassette tape recorder, notebook and three ink pens. Molly and Allison were already drinking a cup of coffee by the time I slung my backpack beside the kitchen chair and graciously accepted the steaming cup that Molly slid across the table.

"Okay," I glanced from one woman to the other, "where do we start?"

Molly began her tale, as Allison interjected various details, forcing me to stop the recording several times. At one point, Molly was standing behind me exasperatedly shaking her head "NO!" while motioning wildly with her arms.

Allison ignored her completely.

"Don't tell me all the sordid particulars of your recent adventures, Allison." I said, when I saw the discomfort it was causing Molly. "Please! I work here, remember?" I released a loud sigh, "Plus, you shouldn't be smoking."

"I am eighty-eight years old. How many years do you think it will take to kill me off?" Allison boisterously smacked her knee.

I frowned in her direction.

"Sorry Carolyn, I'll be quiet."

"Thanks." I tapped record and continued, "Let me get this straight. An Indian woman named Nina raised you?" I inquired with narrowed eyes, "Really?"

"Yep," Molly nodded sincerely.

"Pop pulled you both from a raging river with one hand?" A scrutinizing expression unwillingly crossed my face, "Wow, he must have been strong."

Molly grinned, "He was six-foot-five inches tall and weighed over three hundred fifty pounds," she assured me, "he was a strong man."

"Whoa," I accepted. "Okay. Did Pop ever buy the tractor?"

Molly shook her head, "He didn't. It was several months before Pop returned to Whitmer. He told Nina he could live without a fancy tractor. So, they tilled the garden with their handheld tools, and the horse-drawn plow forever."

I considered her story as I scribbled the details on my notepad. "Let me make sure this is correct," I jiggled my foot in anticipation, "you really fired a shot at United States Rangers?"

"No! I fired the rifle up into the air," she regarded me pensively before insisting, "I didn't aim at them."

My chin dropped as I glanced over my notes, "Truthfully,

did you ever see, with your own eyes, a flying squirrel?"

"Sure," Molly looked at me as if I was crazy, "haven't you?"

"Not that I recall," I confessed.

"Oh, you would remember if you had ever seen a squirrel fly." She guaranteed, adding a twitch of her nose.

I reflected on all she had conveyed, "You didn't realize that Nina and Pop weren't your biological parents until you were practically a teenager. Why do you think this never crossed your mind until Zach mentioned it to you?"

Molly regarded me as though I was as thick as a brick, "Nina and Pop had friends from all over the county, and beyond. None of them had the same color skin, and they might be rich or poor. It didn't matter to them. Nationality, race, religion or social status never crossed my parents' minds. I was reared to pay no mind to what folks looked like, but to what they had inside. Traits like integrity, kindness and respect are what makes up a person." She added as an afterthought, "Plus, there wasn't any proper schooling, so Nina taught me how to read and write, and there were very few influences from the outside world." She exhaled deeply, "It was an easier, more peaceful time."

"Amen." I concurred. "Here is the next question." I looked at her to see if she was following along, "Did the birthing up Tucker Holler influence you concerning sex or having children?"

"Well, Lord have mercy, heck yeah!" Her eyes grew wide, "For a long spell, anyway."

"I bet," I laughed, "did you ever find out if you were related to the folks who lived up Tucker Holler?"

"I have no idea who my birth parents were. It doesn't really matter, and Nina may have known. I thought at one time she rescued me from a potentially bad situation, and fibbed about finding me on the front porch of the cabin in October of 1905." She looked me straight in the eye, "I honestly believe it doesn't matter where you come from because where you're going is all that matters."

"Agreed," I stretched across the table and hit pause. "I just snapped the recording off," I measured her response, "and want to ask this – did Pop and Nina smoke marijuana?"

"You are being presumptuous. It was Kinnikinnik," Molly scowled, "it was one of Nina's special compounds, which was a mixture of plain ole Virginian tobacco and Sage leaves. They only used herbs and spices for medicinal purposes, and Sage is known to strengthen the nervous system, improve memory, and sharpen the senses."

"Fair enough," I accepted, as I examined the landmarks of time that had been conveyed. "So, Nina broke Frank's nose and then dosed him up with a laxative. Would you say this is an accurate portrayal?"

"Yeah," Molly laughingly replied, daring to add, "she could be bad-tempered at times." She bent down and lifted Woody to her lap. "She was always kind to me and Pop, though." The cat brushed his head under her hand and she rhythmically began stroking his back.

So, within a little over four hours, I was up to date on Molly's arrival, the flood, the terrifying lynching, the incident with the United States Rangers, the birthing up Tucker Holler, and of course, Zach Moore. I even jotted down Allison's rendition, concerning their recent adventures, which she encouraged me to include in the memoir.

By the time Molly had diced the eggs and added tiny

slices of celery to the salad, it was almost time for me to scurry out for class. I gobbled down the egg salad sandwich, chased it with some sweet tea, and promised to return the following morning.

"Carolyn, if you want to hang out with us this evening, we will be partying on the patio," Allison offered.

"Hopefully, the police won't be stopping by," I glanced over my shoulder as I placed my dirty dishes in the sink.

Molly forced a laugh as she exchanged glances with Allison. "We are trying a new margarita recipe out after dinner, but I don't think things will get rowdy enough to call in the troops."

Allison nudged me, "Of course you never can tell, but you are invited anytime. We always have plenty of laughter and stories to share."

"I'd better pass on this evening, but I will see you tomorrow morning." I packed my notebook and tape recorder into the side of my backpack. "Oh, and by the way," I told them as I slung the sack over my shoulder, "I do agree with you concerning Mr. Farmer."

"What about Mr. Farmer?" Allison nonchalantly inquired.

"He is a sex-starved maniac," I gave her a wink.

"Good." Allison fiendishly acknowledged, "I've been looking for a decadent man."

"I thought you said you were looking for a *decent* man," Molly corrected.

"At my age," Allison came clean, "I'll have to take what I can get."

Monongahela Mountains, West Virginia
August 8, 1920

Nina handed Molly three Ball jars to carry into the kitchen. "I'll be right in after I fetch some Ginseng," she told her. Molly arranged the jars on the table and washed the countertop with some lye soap, rinsing it carefully with warm water when she had finished. She divided up the spices into two distinct piles and placed a pot of water over the fire.

"We are all set," Nina announced as she pushed in the back door. "Are you ready to review what you've learned?"

"Yep," Molly nodded energetically.

"Okay," Nina place her hand on her hip, "what is this?" She pointed to a full-size plant that had been pulled, root and all, straight from the earth.

"Belladonna," Molly replied with confidence.

"Perfect!" Nina said approvingly. "Is it poisonous?"

"Yes, indeed."

"What part of this plant should be used?"

"The leaf and root, only."

"And," Nina inquired, "what does it help cure?"

Molly squinted her eyes as she considered the options. "Whooping cough."

"Anything else?"

"It can be used to ease pain."

"How should it be administered?" Nina further probed.

"One should use ten to twenty drops of tincture every three to four hours."

"Molly, you are a very smart young woman," Nina complimented, as she selected the perfect knife to use for the forthcoming task.

"Let me ask ya something, Nina. How did you learn so much about medicine?"

Nina's eyes sparkled as she recalled her past, "Traditionally, the Seneca women were experts on gathering plants, roots, berries, and nuts. My grandmother taught me how to use nature's bounty to make medicine and cures."

"Did the Seneca people eat the same things we do?" Molly asked.

Nina eagerly explained, "For the most part, the staple of our diet was called 'the three sisters,' which included corn, beans, and squash. The women in the clan could take these three single vegetables and create dozens of ways to prepare them." Nina pointed to another heap. "Enough about the past, how about this herb?"

"That," Molly rubbed at her chin, "is Butterbar."

"What do we have to remember about Butterbar?"

"It's very rare around these parts, so we have to preserve the seeds in the cellar during the winter, and plant them in wet soil during season."

"Exactly. What do the extracts heal?"

"Headaches?" Molly said, immediately realizing it sounded more like a question than an answer.

Nina gave her a quick wink. "We are going to start working with Ginseng, first." She gently washed the dried root and chose the perfect knife to slice it into thin slivers. "We only harvest the mature plants with red berries," Nina explained. "It can be used as a stimulant, to help cure certain types of diabetes, as an aphrodisiac, and it will help with male dysfunction."

"What's an aphrodisiac and male dysfunction?" Molly curiously inquired.

Nina bit her lip, trying to find the correct words to convey to Molly. "An aphrodisiac will help one get in the mood." She answered, deliberately avoiding the rest of the explanation.

"In the mood for what?"

Nina inhaled deeply. "Sex," she responded frankly.

Molly's thoughts drifted back to the birthing up Tucker Holler and she scrunched her nose in disgust. "And male dysfunction?" she reluctantly probed.

Nina released a hushed sigh, "That's when a man can't *perform* in the bed."

Molly wrestled with this information, "Do men really ask you, *out loud*, for this treatment?" She asked disbelievingly.

Nina became consumed with giggles, "No. Thank God. Usually they just say they're havin' difficulties and then point toward their private parts."

"How embarrassing," Molly mumbled, "I hope no man ever solicits the cure for their private part difficulties from me. My face would turn beet red, and then I would just straight up die of pure discomfiture."

Nina laughed, "Oh, it ain't that bad. Once you get used to it. Besides Molly, I am teaching you everything I know about herbs and their healing properties, just in case you ever need the knowledge. We all have a different purpose in life, and your purpose may have nothin' to do with medicine." She glanced in Molly's direction to see if she was listening. "The struggle in life is to find your own purpose. What God has called you to do, may be entirely different from my callin'."

Molly tilted her head, trying to take everything Nina was explaining to heart.

"You are here to accomplish great things, Molly Minion. Don't ever doubt yourself." She pointed toward the corner of the table, "Could you hand me a jar?"

Molly picked up a cobalt-blue jar to hand to Nina. The residue of the lye soap lingering on her hand caused the jar to slip. She watched in horror as it tumbled, as if in slow motion, to the wooden floor. The jar shattered into hundreds of tiny shards over the floor. Molly froze, and held her breath for a brief moment before breaking out hysterically in tears. "I am so sorry, Nina."

Nina looked at Molly, toward the splintered blue glass covering the floorboards, and back to young woman. "Did you cut yourself?"

Molly shook her head no.

"Why are you crying?"

"I'm so sorry," she sobbed, "I didn't mean to break it."

"I know you didn't mean to break it," Nina studied her.

"But it is one of your favorite blue jars."

"Molly," Nina said at last. She grasped both of the young woman's hands, "It's just a jar. A thing. A nonliving object. It is not important enough for you to feel bad. I assure you."

Molly dipped her head down low.

"Are you alright?"

"I am." Her eyes rose to gauge Nina's reaction.

"Good," Nina let loose of her hands, "I'm gonna grab the broom and we'll get this mishap cleaned up."

"I truly am sorry." Molly apologized again.

Nina held her hand up, "Not another word. This is done, over, and never to be spoken of again."

Although Nina most likely never recalled the incident,

Molly recollected it almost every time she was asked to fetch one of Nina's special blue Ball jars, and made a vow to herself to replace it tenfold.

Springfield Senior Care Facility
1990
"Lessons Learned"

"So, Nina taught you all about herbs, extracts and the proper way to preserve them?" I found myself jiggling my foot so hard I thought it might fall off my leg bone. I always tended to do this when my thoughts were flying through my head too fast to capture.

"Yes, she taught me all kinds of things, like how to treat everyone with respect, the ins and outs of farming, how to conjure up a cure, the value of every living thing, and why one shouldn't get too big for their britches." Molly recalled a menagerie of life lessons, which had been imparted to her by Nina. "She was a wonderful woman who embodied in her own life the loving principles she taught to me."

I placed my hand on my knee, willing it to calm down, "Nina seemed quite educated for a woman during those times."

"I think she learned to read when she lived on a reservation as a child, although she never spoke about her early days. Plus, she owned a dictionary that was so old that half the pages were falling out of it. She enjoyed flipping through the book and discovering new and exotic words. She used to say that all the problems in the world could be solved if folks could learn to read and follow the directions in the Good Book."

"That is probably the truth," I reflected.

"Nina and I would learn new words and use them over

and over until they stuck in our heads. One time we spent an entire week practicing lip movements, we would perch, purse, and pucker our lips contortedly whenever one of us would call out the word."

Molly beamed, as the long lost memory returned to her. "Pop caught on and he kept saying, 'Show me how ya *pucker* your lips, Nina.' Then he would lean forward and give her a big kiss."

She flipped her hand in the air, "I would cover my eyes with my hands and remind them, in mock disgust, that there was a child present, which caused them to break out in laughter. Honestly, to tell you the truth, there is nothing as charming as growing up in a family where love and affection are displayed openly."

"You've had quite a crowded life, with many turns and surprises. Do you feel this is why you can remember the events so vividly?" I doodled on the top of my notepad as she deliberated my question.

"Yeah," she nodded slightly, "probably so."

"So," I blurted out unexpectedly, "what happened to Pop and Nina?"

Molly folded her hands, rested them on the table, and inhaled deeply. Her story came slowly at first, and each word seemed to be torn unwillingly from her mind. It was as if she had suddenly mustered up, a long-lost fragment of a hazy dream.

Monongahela Mountains, West Virginia
November 20, 1925

Molly had finished her classes at Bluefield State College for the day and hurried to the post office to gather her mail. She rarely received anything of importance, but occasionally Nina would send her a letter reminding her of how proud they were that she was attending college, prompting her to concentrate on her studies, and emphasizing how much they missed and loved her. Today, however, there was an envelope in her post office box with Pop's handwriting adorning the front. She slid her finger through the parchment and quickly plucked the notelet from the envelope.

Dear Molly,
Please come home soon. Nina is poorly and we miss you very much.
Love,
Pop

"Poorly?" Molly's face seeped with concern. *"If I contact my professors, I should be able to complete my examinations early, go home, then be back in my classes a few days after Thanksgiving break."*

She went about making plans to leave the campus, as soon as she possibly could, so she could get back up on the mountaintop to be with Nina and Pop. *"Home. The only place I want to be."*

When she arrived back on top of the mountain, she

consciously appreciated the way her hot breath quickly turned to steam in the chill of the country air. The mud covered paths, and sleeping orchard even brought her delight. *"Was that a flying squirrel?"* She turned her ear up as she heard the soft swishing sound vibrate through the air. The barren trees that stood stout and leafless reminded her that winter had set in prematurely this season. The farm seemed more precious than she remembered, and she was relieved to notice that things hadn't seemed to change since she had left, nearly fourteen months earlier.

She didn't bother knocking on the door to announce her arrival, because she knew Nina could hear her coming from a mile away, and after all, this was her home. She twisted the door handle and pushed into the cabin. The spicy scent of wood crackling in the big fireplace filled her heart with brilliant memories.

"Pop? Nina?" She scanned the cabin, "Are you here?" Molly called out.

"On the back porch," she heard Pop bellow.

When Molly slid through the back door, she was shocked to see the state of Nina. She and Pop were snuggled up in quilts, each in their own rocking chair. Pop rose and walked over to give Nina a big hug, while Nina smiled dimly from her seated position. Molly noticed Nina's right eyelid was drooping on one side and when she smiled at Molly, only one side of her mouth moved. She had lost a considerable amount of weight, and her eyes seemed cloudy.

"What are the two of you doing outside in this chilly weather?" Molly chastised.

"We just decided to come out and get a quick breath of fresh air, and partake in a dose of Nina's medication." He offered Molly a quick wink. "Have a seat and join us for a spell."

Molly pulled up a wooden chair and plopped down on it, sliding it to Nina's side. "Are you feeling poorly, Nina?"

"I've felt better," Nina released a dry cough, "and seeing you sure brightens my spirits. I am so glad you were able to make it home." Nina stretched out her hand and patted Molly's arm. "Would you like to join us?"

"Join you?" Molly teased.

Pop struck a match and lit the pipe and handed it to Molly. They passed it back and forth a few times before Nina inquired.

"What can you smell, Pop?"

"The hog pen." He chuckled.

"How about you, Molly?"

"The wood smoke from the chimney," she whispered.

"What can you hear?" Nina asked.

"The breeze rustling through the trees." Pop offered up.

"The love in your voices," Molly confided.

"Tell me something you'll always remember feeling," she probed.

"Holding you close to me." He winked at his wife.

Nina gasped in mock surprise, "Pop, you are ornery. Molly is sitting right here."

A chortle escaped from his throat. "Molly is old enough to know that I love you." His eyes twinkled as he gazed at Nina. "You are a good wife, Nina Minion."

"You are a fine husband, Pop."

"You are the best parents a girl could ever want," Molly chimed in.

Pop puffed up, as he and Nina exchanged glances, "You are the most remarkable blessing to come into our lives, Molly Minion."

"Amen," Pop bellowed loudly.

The tears poured down Molly's cheeks, as she soulfully comprehended how lucky she was to have these two wonderful people as her kin, and silently thanked God for their presence in her life.

Later that evening, Molly snuggled in by Nina's side on the bed and held her hand. "Can I fix you anything?"

"No," Nina's eyes cracked open as she pointed toward a chest of drawers in the corner, "but could you fetch my brooch?"

"Sure," Molly walked over and quickly found it carefully positioned on a crocheted handkerchief. "Do you want me to fasten it to your shirt?"

"No," Nina shook her head, "I want you to have it."

"I can't accept your brooch, Nina. It's the only precious thing you've ever had in your life."

Nina's nose wrinkled with incredulity, "The only precious thing I've ever had? What are you talking about? I've had all kinds of precious, beautiful things in my lifetime. The birds, the wildflowers, I've held hundreds of newborns, and you are the most beautiful present I have ever received." She thoughtfully considered, "And of course, I had Pop. All gifts from God."

"Pop is one of the most beautiful things you've had in your life?" Molly was pulling her leg.

"Of course," Nina giggled, "he is as cute as a bug in a rug."

Molly leaned over and whispered into Nina's ear, "A very *large* bug."

Pop's head appeared from around the crook of the kitchen, "I heard that!" He chuckled, before disappearing back behind the curve in the wall.

The women started laughing hysterically and Nina covered her mouth, as she so often did lately, when she smiled. Molly imagined it was because she was ashamed of her teeth, and she didn't quite understand the notion, because she felt Nina had a beautiful, soulful smile. It didn't matter if a tooth was missing.

Nina had taken it upon herself, after several months of self-doctoring, to extract one of her bottom teeth, three winters ago, when the infection had become unbearable. Besides, Nina's smile was more of the way her eyes wrinkled up at the corners when she was happy.

"You're a wonderful daughter, Molly Minion."

"You are a wonderful mama, Nina Minion."

They sat in silence as their eyes contemplated one another, each of them, fully comprehending the affection, love and devotion they shared.

Two nights later, Nina died quietly in her sleep. She died with Pop holding her in his arms. He held her through the night and when the sun rose the following morning, he unwillingly let her go.

Molly and Pop mourned together, and they mourned alone. For two days they wept, wailed, bawled and fitfully slept from pure emotional exhaustion.

Once, Molly had peered out the window to see Pop violently pounding on the ground beside the barn in the pouring rain. She flew out the door and squatted down beside him. "Pop, please come in the house," she tried to lift him up, "and let me fix you some tea."

"Molly," Pop confessed between muted cries, "I'm not sure I can stay here without the love of my life. My heart has a hole that is so big, a bull could pass clean through it."

"You're just mourning, Pop." She sat down in the mud

beside him, "Time will help heal the pain."

It was impossible to distinguish between the tears and the raindrops, as the skies cried along with them, seemingly appreciating, all which had been lost.

The night before Nina's burial, Pop pulled Molly to his side and gently kissed the top of her head. "Come sit beside me." He patted the bed as a sad smile crawled up, underneath his moustache. "Molly Minion, I love you very much, and Nina loved you, too. You have made us so very proud. Ever since you were delivered to our doorstep, I have praised the Lord every single day of my life. Ya know, Molly? Out of all the people in this big ole world, God blessed me. Can you believe it? God blessed me."

She patted his hand affectionately, "You deserve to be blessed, Pop. You're a good man."

"Molly?" He asked conspiratorially, "Let me ask ya something."

"Sure."

"Do you remember years ago, when Frank Moore fell down the steps and broke his nose?"

"Yep."

"Had he hurt you?"

"No." Molly recalled, *"Not physically."*

"Did Nina have anything to do with his unfortunate accident?"

Molly remembered the day very vividly. *"Don't tell Pop,"* Nina had told her as she rushed out the door with rifle in hand. "I did not witness nothin'." Molly winked.

"That's what I figured." He grinned warmly as he handed his worn Bible to Molly and whispered, "I wish I had more to give to you."

"Oh, Pop. You and Nina gave me a glorious life. I could

never repay you." She fingered through the worn pages of his black leather Bible, "Do you want me to read to you?"

"No," his mouth curved up faintly, "I want you to keep it."

"I can't keep your Bible, Pop." She placed it on the bed beside him, "You are going to need the Good Book to help you adjust to Nina's death."

"There's a letter tucked inside," he tapped his finger on the cover. "Nina left it for me," he paused, "and for you."

Molly sang a sweet song to him, over and over again, as he drifted in and out of sleep.

Why should I feel discouraged,
Why should the shadows come.
Why should my heart feel lonely,
And long for heaven and home.

I sing because I'm happy,
I sing because I'm free.
For His eye is on the sparrow,
And I know He watches me.

When he finally floated into a full state of slumber, she tucked his Bible under his hand and kissed him on the cheek. "I love you, Pop."

The following morning, as the rooster announced the arrival of the day, Molly climbed out of bed, wiped the sleep from her eyes and stumbled over to the teapot. She heaped a few teaspoons of black tea in a strainer, located the cinnamon bread, and pulled three brown eggs from the icebox. Although she was dreading burying Nina today, she was determined to help Pop make it through. "Pop? Are you awake? How do you want your eggs cooked this morning?"

Pop didn't answer her, so she walked to the edge of the cabin where he and Nina had, years before, made a makeshift wall to partition off their bedroom. "Pop?" She gently nudged his shoulder. "Pop?" She rolled the big old man over. She could see he was in perfect peace. "Pop? You didn't leave me? Did ya?" She knew the answer. She rested her head on his chest and lay there with him for a long time before gliding the Bible from his hand and opening it to a location marked by a yellowed piece of parchment. She plucked Nina's letter from the book of Matthew and silently read the message.

Dear Pop and Molly,

I want to thank you for making my life so complete. You have given me joy, love, and made all my dreams come true. The kindness and tenderness you have shown me is more than I ever deserved. I love you with all of my heart, and want you to know I will be watching over you until the time comes when you join me in our Lord's heaven. When you hear the sparrows sing their lovely song, or smell the sweet scent of wildflowers, I will be there. When you feel discouraged, I will be with you. When you laugh, I will be laughing with you.

There is one important item that you need to tend to for me. I have buried several Ball jars beside the herb garden. These jars contain money and other treasures that I have saved over the years, in case of an emergency. I have drawn a map, which is enclosed, so they will be easy to find. Remember Pop, your stride is longer than mine, so take tiny steps when you go to locate them.

Please always keep me close in your heart.

You are my joy.
It has been a delight to spend my life with you.
Love,
Nina

Molly fingered the parchment as she stared at Nina's shotgun. She wasn't ready to smile Pop and Nina away. She cried for a long spell, before opening the map left by Nina. She gasped when she realized Nina had buried a myriad of jars over the years. *"You sweet, smart, brave woman."* She covered her mouth to suppress a cry that was attempting to leap from her heart. She cried for Nina. She cried for Pop. *"You big, kind, generous, galoot. What am I going to do without you both?"*

Molly poured herself a cup of tea and shuffled to the front porch where she plopped down into Pop's rocking chair and fixed her eyes out toward the great horizontal rents opening in the purple clouds that glowed scarlet like the poppies that burst forth each summer. Soon a slice of rising sun squinted through these sky pockets and glinted in each morning dew droplet on every blade of grass and twig in the trees. Molly languished silently, taking in the scents, the beauty and the melancholy of the forest. She thought of those she had lost. She thought of Pop, of Nina, and of Zach Moore.

A wave of anger unexpectedly enveloped her, *"Folks just abandon me on this old porch all the time,"* she thought, as she recalled the story of her arrival. The rage, sorrow, and pain she was feeling burst unexpectedly from her throat. She screamed, her voice echoing down the mountain, "Why did you leave me?" Her gaze searched the sky. She stood motionless, listening, as if waiting for a response.

A mighty gust suddenly stirred in from nowhere, and the fallen leaves circled around on the ground, as the limbs of the trees sloped sidelong. A mislaid Ball jar that had been propped on the porch railing tumbled to the ground.

Then, just as quickly as the puff arrived, it vanished.

Molly blankly stared at the cracked jar before bending over to pick it up, carefully removing the Lady Smock leaves from inside the fractured glass. *"Lady Smock,"* she grinned, *"the cure for a broken heart."*

Monongahela Mountains, West Virginia
November 26, 1925

Molly spent Thanksgiving morning alone. She busied herself with cleaning and tidying up the cabin. As she worked, she found notes tucked under jars, in the creases of pillows, in skillets, and even in the icebox.

"Make sure Pop takes his Goatsfoot every evening or his gout will flair up."

"Only use the above ground parts of the Horsetail."

"The spare Ball jars are in the top shelf of the smokehouse."

"Make sure you read the Bible."

Dozens of torn pieces of paper were slipped in the most unusual places, and they just kept turning up. *"Thank you for the reminder,"* Molly would say aloud each time she discovered a new message. Molly spied a slip of paper crammed in the top of a jar packed with Lavender. She twisted the lid open and the scent of dried spring blossoms was so cloyingly sweet she could almost taste them. *"God will help you find your way if you seek Him."* Molly sighed, "Yeah, I hope so, Nina."

Molly wrapped Nina's tethered jacket around her shoulders, snatched up an old quilt, and tucked herself under the apple tree. She dropped down on the frosty earth and curiously examined the map left behind by Nina. She located the shovel, walked to the east corner of the smokehouse, and took the exact number of steps indicated on the map before examining the earth closely. She began to tap a section of the ground with her shoe. *"This has to be the spot."*

She put her back into the digging, thrusting the shovel hard and deep into the earth. The hole grew deep, and Molly was about to give up when the blade of the shovel finally struck something. A familiar cracking sound caused her to frown. *"I'm going to have to be more careful,"* she thought. She tossed away the shovel and went to her knees to carefully brush away the remaining dirt with her hands, careful not to cut herself on the broken Ball jar. Picking away the slivers of glass and tossing them in a heap, she scraped the red clay earth away, only to discover a wadded bundle of cash.

Molly took exactly thirteen steps toward the apple tree, swept the damp, matted cottonwood away with her foot, and jabbed the shovel cautiously into the dirt. She then scraped the soil away in layers, careful not to disturb anything, or worse, break another one of Nina's jars. When she spied the golden colored lid, she dug it out using her hands, wound the lid open and slid a piece of parchment from its belly. The edges were aged and turning brown, almost crumbling in her hands, as she unfolded the document. It was a deed. The deed to the farm. Five-hundred and four acres, marked clearly by witness trees in all four corners, and it had been given to Nina as a wedding gift, back in December of 1905. This was back when people of American Indian descent were not allowed to own land in West Virginia. The most recent inscription indicated that Nina and Pop had imparted the land to Molly three months earlier.

Molly paused to wipe a smear of mud from her cheek. *"Why did I decide to unearth these jars when the soil is half frozen? I should have waited for more favorable weather."*

She was about to search for the next buried treasure

when she heard a horse approaching from the South. She paused, wondering if she should grab the shotgun, then decided she wouldn't carry a gun around all the time like Nina had done. After all, it was 1925, and she was living in a civilized society. *"I think I'll fetch it just in case,"* she reconsidered. The screen door slapped shut behind her just as the man pulled on the bit collar of his horse. This stranger was a welcoming sight and her spirits rose high.

"Howdy, Ma'am." He provided a polite tilt of his head. He gazed admiringly at the woman, a slender creature garbed in a plain brown dress, and worn leather jacket. "I am looking for Ms. Nina."

"Nina passed away recently."

"I'm so sorry to hear 'bout that."

"Thank ya, kindly." Molly's hand rose to cover her eyes from the glare of the cloudless wintry sky. "Is there something I can help ya with?"

"Well, I'm not quite sure." He glimpsed down toward the weapon she had slung casually at her hip. "My name is Loyal Smith and I rode up here to inquire about buying some of her remedies for a store I'm planning on opening."

"Do you have any particular compounds in mind?"

He pressed his lips together as if in deep concentration, "No. I don't know enough about 'em to rightly say."

Molly smiled at his honest confession. "Do you know what symptoms you might be looking to cure?"

"Probably about anything folks might need fixed," he pointed toward her rifle. "Do you mind if I hop down for a minute."

He was a handsome man, about her age, and his kind eyes, blonde hair, and fair skin made her feel comfortable. Her instincts indicated that he was a fine person and his presence didn't disturb her like some folks did. "Sure," she nodded, "can I fix you some sweet tea?"

"Thank ya. I'd be much obliged." He grinned sincerely.

Loyal dismounted, loosely tied the reins of his horse around the fence post and waited outside on the porch until Molly reappeared carrying two drinking jars.

"So, Mr. Smith," she handed him a glass, "you're looking to purchase some herbal medicines."

"Yes, Ma'am." He took a long satisfying drink of his tea. "I don't think I caught your name."

"I didn't offer it." Molly could tell by his expression he was taken aback, so she quickly interjected, "My name is Molly. Molly Minion."

"Please to meet ya, Mrs. Minion."

"Miss," Molly corrected.

"Even better," he said as a cunning grin formed on his face. "Do you know anything about the treatments Nina prepared?"

Molly looked at him as if he had lost his mind, "Of course." She squared her shoulders. "Nina taught me everything about 'em. I know what the remedy is for digestive problems, gout, back pain, fever, jaundice, insomnia, infections, and heart problems. You name it, and I can conjure it up."

"Wonderful," he stared intently into her eyes.

Molly turned away, feeling flustered, not understanding why these unfamiliar feelings were stirring.

"Can I call on you?" He asked in deep voice.

"Call on me for what?" She looked questioningly at him.

Something about the way he said it, his voice hushed and husky, his breath coming fast, let her know that his question came from a source much deeper than curiosity concerning herbal remedies.

"Well," his attention dropped to his boots, "the way a man generally calls on a woman."

"Oh," she managed to squeak out, "that'd be fine."

His lips parted in a radiant smile that crinkled his deep blues eyes at the corners. "Thank ya. How about I stop by next week and you could provide me with a list of possible compounds I can buy for my store, and I'll bring some lunch when I come, too. This way we will be able to mix business with pleasure."

Molly could feel her palms getting damp from nerves. "A woman could get a bad reputation asking a man into her home without a chaperone being present," she replied frankly.

He understood how quickly vicious rumors could spread. "Okay, I'll stop by next Thursday to discuss the possibility of buying some of your products, and then escort you to dinner in a public place. Does this sound more reputable?"

"Yes, it does. I would be very pleased to accompany you."

"Perfect," he handed the empty drinking glass to her. "I'll see you next week then."

Molly watched him walk back to his horse, still grinning fetchingly, as he turned and waved goodbye.

It wasn't more than an hour later, that Molly suddenly perceived the sound of a herd of wagons rolling up the mountain path. She snatched up Nina's shotgun and stood on the porch, only to spy the preacher with his wife and children, several wagons full of folks from Tucker Holler, and the Osborne clan parading toward her front door.

"We figured you best not be alone during the holiday season," the preacher announced as the kids hopped down from the platform.

She greeted the crowd warmly, as they climbed from their carriages, each family offering bundles of food. "We decided to celebrate Thanksgiving at the Minion farm," Mrs. Osborne explained, as she handed over a crate filled with meat and extra eating utensils.

Molly stood, jaw gaping open, as the community continued to set up a full Thanksgiving feast, with all the fixings. After grace was given, they feasted on ham, potatoes garnished with tiny slices of ramps, cornbread, green beans smothered in bacon grease, fried okra, collard greens, deviled eggs, and blackberry cobbler. Molly beamed with delight as she took in the details of each story the folks shared with her about Pop and Nina.

The sound of laughter filled the air, as the fiddles played, and the voices of folks singing drifted like a warm blanket of hope over the farmhouse. When twilight swept below the mountaintop, her friends left, just as unexpectedly as they had arrived, and Molly had smiled them away, as the horses carried the diverse crowd back down the frozen path. She realized the gratitude in her heart could never be fully spoken, and was truly thankful for the friendship and legends they had shared with her on this most unforgettable Thanksgiving Day.

When the sun towered over the mountain on the following morning, Molly again set out poking, prodding, and digging throughout the yard, herb garden, and alongside the rickety barn. Much later that evening, she figured she had uncovered each of the items marked on the drawing left by Nina. She stood inquisitively staring at the kitchen table where heaped up items, from each of the jars, lay unearthed and exposed. Thousands of dollars, one indistinguishable blob, sixteen rings, a diminutive swan-neck pair of scissors, eight jeweled necklaces, a few gold teeth, which Molly reasoned was mighty odd, two watches, a small tattered book filled with recipes used for medicinal purposes, and of course, the deed to the farm which had been bestowed to her.

"This is my legacy," she appreciated, as she traced her finger lightly over the assortment of excavated relics bequeathed to her. "Thank you, Nina," Molly whispered. She turned her ear up to listen, *"You are welcome,"* she romanticized.

Springfield Senior Care Facility
1990
"Precious Heirlooms"

"Alright Carolyn," Allison snapped her fingers to get my attention, "do you want a cup of coffee or a Bloody Mary?"

I glanced up from my notebook, "It's too early to be drinking alcoholic beverages, give me a coffee."

Allison shook her head as if she was disgusted, "Youth is wasted on the young," she cleverly quoted George Bernard Shaw.

"Coffee, please." I reiterated, as my concentration turned to Molly. "Let's fast forward to today," I suggested. "How did you end up at Springfield Care Facility?"

"Oh," Molly provided a quick wave of her hand. "I just decided to retire and relax. This place is beautiful, and I don't have to worry about falling down, breaking a hip, and having no one around to help me up."

"What did you do with the farm?"

"I still own five-hundred and four acres right smack dab in the middle of Monongahela National Forest."

"That's amazing," I thought, "I didn't realize individuals could own property within the boundaries of National Parks or Forests."

"You can if you refuse to sell out."

"Did you return to college?"

"No, I stayed there."

"How did you manage to make a living, way up in the middle of nowhere?"

Molly joyfully confessed, "With herbs and spices." She nonchalantly shrugged her shoulders. "I am the owner of

Mountain State Herbal Remedies."

"You own *the* Mountain State Herbal Remedies?" Allison's jaw plunged open. "The world renowned company? That's remarkable!"

Molly slanted her head slightly, "Not really. Since Nina taught me all the particulars concerning herbs and elixirs, along with their properties and tinctures. All I had to do was package and market them."

"No, I mean it is remarkable that I just bought Bladderwrack powder for my arthritis and paid three dollars to have it shipped. My best friend and next-door neighbor is the owner of Mountain State Herbal Remedies, and I paid three dollars for shipping," Allison released a loud sigh. "I am officially requesting a refund for my shipping costs," she set her chin.

"I don't feel that is fair, Allison." I interjected. "It's not as if Molly is conjuring up the remedies right here in her kitchen." I reconsidered the two women's recent history, "Are you?"

"Of course not," Molly rolled her eyes. "But, I do have jars of all of my products tucked in the cabinet." She tilted her head toward the tall, mahogany cupboard standing staunchly against the living room wall.

Our gaze followed her direction, "Can we see them?" I curiously inquired.

"Sure," she motioned for us to follow her. She swung the doors open with magnificent flair, and we stood staring at dozens of cobalt Ball jars, packed full of herbs, extracts, and tinctures.

I noticed a lovely doll adorned with an auburn lace trimmed dress. Its smooth porcelain face reminded me of delicate brown eggs. The doll looked like Molly. The color of her eyes, and the hue of her skin, matching. "Beautiful," I whispered in awe, as I ran my finger delicately over the crack in her knee.

"Look here," Molly reached for a cloth resting on the top shelf, "here is Nina's brooch." She carefully unwrapped an aged handkerchief, presenting the tiny green stones that reminded me of sparkling emeralds.

"It is exquisite."

"Thank you," she folded the corners of the hanky back around the trinket. "And," she presented with great elegance, a tiny tethered notebook, "this journal contains the formulas and instructions for creating each of the remedies sold by my company." She giggled, "There are some ancient potions inscribed in here that are now banned. Obviously, I don't package or sell those."

"So," I supposed, "are you an herbologist?"

"Yeah, I guess you could say herbology is my chosen field." Molly motioned toward the sofa and we sat down. Woody the tabby cat jumped into my lap and rubbed his nose against the brown leather-covered book. I carefully fingered through the worn pages admiring the drawings that accompanied the directions. "Nina was quite an artist, too."

"Yes, she was good at everything."

"Did you ever determine what caused her death?" I asked.

"Lyme disease, I believe. It was discovered a few years ago. When I learned the symptoms linked to Lyme disease, I realized this must have been what triggered Nina's death."

"Lyme Disease is caused by tick bites, right?"

"Yes," Molly confirmed, "and the mountains in West

Virginia have deer ticks everywhere. I can't recall a summer that Nina didn't examine my hair every evening searching for, and plucking out, the little blood suckers."

"Pop died so soon after Nina's death," I questioned, "what do you think caused his death?"

"I reckon he died from a broken heart." Molly folded her shaking hands in her lap, as her gaze fell to the floor. "He loved Nina dearly," she whispered as she used her fingers to smooth out the skin on her forehead. I saw a shiny film across her eyes, the beginning of tears. "I still miss them both, very much."

"Molly, I don't believe you said – did you ever marry?"

"Oh," she waved her hand nonchalantly, "almost."

Monongahela Mountains, West Virginia
December 25, 1925

Molly decided to throw caution to the wind, and disregard any gossip that might come about by inviting a man to join her for Christmas dinner, without a chaperone being present. She heard his horse crunching through the newly fallen snow, several moments before he arrived, and she glanced around the room nervously, double-checking to see if anything was out of place.

"Take your boots off and warm them by the fire," she offered when he stepped over the threshold into the warm, cinnamon scented cabin, "let me fix ya a glass of buttermilk."

"Thank you, Molly, sounds delicious." Loyal took a sip of the buttermilk Molly had just poured him and felt life seep back into his bones. He couldn't remember the last time he'd sat beside a fire in his stocking feet. He fingered the ring he had tucked in his front shirt pocket, and inquisitively inspected the clean, well-built cabin.

"I decided to cook up some stew and cinnamon bread for dessert. It's nothing fancy, just warm and filling for this cold winter day. I hope this is alright." Molly self-consciously walked to the fireplace and busied herself by poking at the fire a couple times to keep the embers burning.

"I'm sure it will be a whole lot better than the meals I cook for myself," Loyal laughed. His eyes turned from the fire and he stared at her. The sight of the beautiful young woman stirring a hearty stew, pouring his milk, and tending to the fireplace made his heart sing. The aroma of fresh yeast rising from the cinnamon batter filled the air, and the steamed buttermilk warmed his stomach. He watched admiringly as she covered the bowl with a dishtowel and placed the batter on the hearth to rise. Her face was framed with soft russet curls, and her eyes, by a set of long black lashes. Her intelligent eyes met his in unwavering assessment. When she smiled at him, he could hardly contain his excitement and almost blurted out the words instinctively.

They had been courting for almost a month now, and as they had spent time sharing stories, she had taught him some of her secrets of how to take an herbal ingredient and conjure up most any natural remedy one could need. In this short time together he had fallen, head over heels, in love with Molly Minion.

"How was your day, Molly?"

"Very busy," she didn't want to admit she had spent hours cleaning, cooking, and primping in front of Nina's mirror, in preparation for their dinner.

"How about you? Did you have a good day?"

"Well," Loyal said without preliminaries, "I did receive some unfortunate news, a few days back, which I want to talk to you about." He patted the couch, inviting her to join him.

"Go on," Molly replied, as she seated herself beside him. She straightened the crease in her skirt before making eye contact.

He leaned close to her, "I received a letter from my mother a couple days ago, and she explained that my father is very ill. She requested I come home to help out with the ranch until they can get everything sorted out." He gulped deeply, "So, I was wondering if you might want to accompany me to Texas?" His eyes widened as he anticipated her response.

"Texas?" Molly's gut seemed to jump into her mouth, as her tremulous smile quickly fell to a frown. "Well," she cleared her throat, trying to will back the tears that were forming, "I don't know." Her hand motioned around the cabin, "I have the farm to tend to, and of course, my medicines…" her voice trailed off.

"Of course, we would get married first," Loyal insisted.

"Are you asking me to wed ya?" Molly's face flushed, and her eyes closed. "Oh, don't ask such a thing yet, Loyal. I'm not sure I ever want to get married. We should strengthen our friendship before we consider marriage."

He pulled the gold ring from his pocket, bent to one knee, and sincerely requested, "May I have your hand in marriage, Molly Minion?"

She was speechless, confused, and she didn't know what to say. She had no desire to leave this farm, or this mountain, as she was perfectly content with her life, just as it was. *"Do I love him?"* Her mind was racing. She could easily ascertan the disappointed expression that dripped from Loyal's face. "I don't know, Loyal." She squeaked out, "I fancy you quite a bit, but I'm not quite sure I want to move half way across the United States." She touched his hand tenderly, "You do understand, don't ya?" He rose back up to the couch and grasped both of her hands.

"I'll make you a good husband," he promised.

"I know you will be a wonderful husband," she bit nervously at her lip, "it's just that I'm surprised, is all. I wasn't expecting a proposal tonight."

Loyal nodded his head slightly, "Fair enough. I hope you can make up your mind soon, because I will be leaving

West Virginia in a little over a week."

"A week?" Molly's hand rose to cover her heart. "Well...well...this is a big decision, Loyal."

"I know." His attention turned toward the fireplace, "Please think it over." She could see a tear form in the corner of his eye. He placed his arm lightly over her shoulders, "I love you."

For several long moments, the only noise in the room was the loud ticking of the mantel clock, its measured sounds mingled with Loyal's resonant breathing. Molly suddenly stood up, walked to the fireplace, and warmly suggested, "Let's enjoy this stew. What do you say?"

Their dinner was as delightful as it could be, considering the uncomfortable circumstances encircling the evening. They made small talk, discussing herbs, spices, and the price of cattle, and when she sliced the cinnamon bread and filled their cups for dessert, she impulsively sprinkled a dash of Ginseng into his after-dinner tea.

Molly offered her hand to him, and he took it eagerly.

Loyal left for Texas the following week, unwillingly leaving her behind.

Molly Minion was alone, once again, with nothing but a smokehouse filled with Ball jars, and her passion for healing.

Springfield Senior Care Facility
1990
"Herbs and Spices"

"Let me get this straight" I inhaled deeply, "you sprinkled a touch of Ginseng into Loyal's tea?"

"I did," she perched her lips together tightly, "I admit it." She sighed deeply, "I'm not proud," she leaned in closer, "but, I ain't ashamed either."

I eyed her incredulously before clarifying, "The aphrodisiac, right?" My mouth gaped open in wonder, "Did it work?"

"Oh yeah," a scheming smile spanned her face, "it worked just fine."

"Do you want to share the details?" Allison probed.

"Nope," Molly adamantly concluded. "Some things are best left private."

"Okay, I only have a few things to wrap up," I snatched up a fresh ink pen, "what was the indistinguishable blob that you uncovered during your quest?"

Molly's eyes grew wide, "Oh!" Her hand rose to cover her mouth, "I found it described in Nina's notes, and have no idea how she came across it, or why she decided to keep it. However, it is Monkshood Root, it's still in there in the cabinet." She pointed in the general direction, "It is a Chinese herb that is highly toxic, and quickly absorbed through the skin." She shrugged her shoulders, "I never unfastened the jar, because she had scratched on the top of the lid, DO NOT OPEN, but I do know it causes cardiac arrest which quickly leads to death."

I stared at her blankly for several long moments, as I searched for a lighter topic, "Okay then." I drew a line through Monkshood Root, figuring I would decide later if I should tell all of Nina's secrets. "I would assume you have made a great deal of money since you are the owner of Mountain State Herbal Remedies. Have you been involved in much philanthropy work?"

"Of course!" Molly chimed. "Mostly local work. For example, when I first started earning money, I helped build new houses for the folks who live up Tucker Holler and founded a free clinic at the mouth of the road."

"Amazing," I acknowledged.

"I have established shelters to help families who are escaping abusive homes," she stared at the ceiling for a moment, "helped to build schools in some of the rural and poorer areas across the state, and of course," she added a devoted wave of her hand, "I tithe."

Allison immediately interrupted Molly, "Ya see, Carolyn! She *should* refund me the three dollars I paid for the shipping of that Bladderwrack!"

Molly and I exchanged knowing glances, as Allison plopped two Bloody Marys down on the table, "Unbelievable," she murmured under her breath as she haphazardly tossed the celery stalks into the glasses.

I purposely disregarded Allison's request for a refund, "Did you stay true to Nina's creations, or did you alter the compounds over the years?"

Molly drummed her fingers on the tabletop as she drifted back in time, "I kept some and I changed a few. Herbal alchemy became my life."

Monongahela Mountains, West Virginia
April 5, 1926

    The first signal of the springtime bonanza coming to the mountains was when the elm trees near the river showed a dim hint of color. Molly had noticed out by the cold mountain swamp, some Skunk Cabbage pushing up its quaint green cap with a purple pedestal inside, and she had delicately cupped her hands around its petals to examine it closely.

    Nina had taught her how to keep a sharp eye open to spot the fragrant pink and white flowers of Trailing Arbutus peeking out from under the leaves flattened by winter snows. Over a period of the last two weeks, the woods had become a fascinating kaleidoscope of colors and a paradise of magnificent spring wildflowers since the warm rain showers had begun to tumble from the sky.

    Thousands of yellow, pink, and purple flowers, pushing through the dense brown leaves carpeted the mountainside, and Molly couldn't take a step without trampling the cheerful blossoms. Intermingled with the blossoming plants, yellow-green ferns grew lavishly in damp areas tucked underneath the large oak trees, and Molly paused to examine the newly developing leaves.

    On this drizzling morning when the sun rivaled with intermittent showers for control of the weather, Molly had wavered about going for a walk, but the skies cleared to some extent, so she set out for the highest peak. She noticed a Mayapple, or Mazyapple, as Nina used to call it, blooming its large white bud from underneath its umbrella-like leaves. She paused for a moment to steal a whiff from its bloom. She made her way through the dense woods and clinging vegetation to where the sky suddenly opened up and a breeze whisked her hair when she reached its highest peak. She lifted her chin and breathed deeply of the moist air that spread through her body like one of Nina's elixirs.

From her vantage point above the thick forest, she watched as the sun fully peeped out from behind its cloud cover, sending rays of brilliant light through the parting trees. The forest rang with the sound of singing birds, squirrels swooshing about, and the occasional scampering of raccoons and groundhogs seeking a hiding place as she interrupted their morning routines.

Today was the day. The day she would decide what to do with her life. She had been praying and listening for guidance from God, and figured the closer she was to the heavens, the louder His voice might be. So, she stepped up onto a tree that had been toppled over by the force of the winter winds, and contemplated her life, her choices, and her future. She fully realized she had no regrets concerning Loyal's proposal, and her refusal to wed him. Even though she had enjoyed his company, she knew Texas was not where she wanted to live her life.

She had spent the winter months reading Nina's notes, and practicing with various extracts, absorbedly learning all that she could about the many mixtures Nina had shared with her over the years.

"Should I find my kin folk?" She pondered. *"Who would that be?"* She stared up toward the heavens. *"Nina's family at the reservation? Pop's kinfolk in Scotland? The folks up Tucker Holler?"* Her gaze lowered down to the mountain, as she fully accepted the fact that her family was gone from

this world. *"The Minion clan,"* she recalled Pop's declaration, *"and I am the only one left."* She desperately prayed, once again, for guidance before lifting her hands to the skies, "Please show me the way, Lord!"

No sooner than the words escaped her mouth, a thought forcefully pushed its way into her mind. *"Herbal alchemy."* She tilted her head up to listen. Had she heard a voice? Or was it a prompting from within? *"Am I knowledgeable enough to create new tinctures?"* "Not yet," she murmured. *"How can I learn more?"* It was during this private conversation with God, that Molly presumed she had been shown the direction her life should follow. Her calling was, after all this time searching, exactly what she had been reared to do, create medicinal compounds for folks needing to be healed.

Springfield Senior Care Facility
1990
"Travels"

"I realized my life had been too comfortable up on top of the mountain, and decided I should travel and learn more about extracts, herbs, and medicine, so I packed my bags and headed straight to Haiti."

I must say I was surprised to learn she was so courageous, "Alone?"

"Yep," she bit at her bottom lip and smiled confidently, "I went to the glorious country of Haiti in 1926 and lived there for two years."

"Did you enjoy your time there?" I asked.

"Of course, she enjoyed her time there," Allison interjected, "who wouldn't?"

"Allison," I sighed, "this is Molly's memoir. Let's allow her to reflect on her visit, okay?"

"Fine," Allison huffed, as she rose from her seat and walked to the sink, "I'll just keep my mouth shut and wash up the dishes."

"I'll get to those later, Allison. Don't fret over them."

Allison peeked over her shoulder, "No. I insist. You fixed us up some great snacks, so the least I can do is clean up the mess." She hastily pushed the plug into the sink, added a dollop of dish liquid, and turned the water on.

Molly thought for a moment. "What did you ask me?"

"About Haiti," I reminded her.

"Of course. I lived near the market place in Port-au-Prince and traveled throughout the country, meeting folks and inquiring about their herbal cures. The people who lived there were good, kind, God fearing folks, and perhaps the most polite, gentle creatures on this planet. It was an amazing experience."

"What did you learn during your stay?" I found myself nervously jiggling my leg, again.

"I learned how to tie gorgeous head wraps," she guaranteed. "The fabric the women in Haiti used was dyed using roots of native plants and the colors were simply brilliant."

"Did you learn anything about folk medicine while you were there?"

Once again, she regarded me as if I was six shy of a dozen. "Of course. They call it leaf-doctoring, and it is an integral part of many Haitians' health care regimens. Since Haitians had very limited access to the attentions of doctors during those days, their reliance on leaf-doctoring was essential to remedying their sicknesses. By listening to them, going along into the woods when they gathered, and reading about their native tropical plants, I learned a great deal."

Our attention turned to Allison who was noisily clanking the glasses around in the sink. Molly and I made a knowing, pointed eye contact before she continued. "There were two particular substances that I continue to use today. One is Sarsaparilla, which is a root that is used as a blood purifier to promote a cleansing action in the bowels, spleen, liver and kidneys. Haitians dose themselves with a tea of Sarsaparilla root to purify their bodies. The second purifier I learned about surprised me. It was Catnip. Have you ever seen Woody lolling around blissfully on a pile of Catnip?" She asked. "He knows this herb makes him feel good. Right?"

I nodded in agreement.

"The folks from Haiti used Catnip for the soothing effect it is known to have on infants. Since it is a mild herb, it is safe to give to babies in the form of tea. They felt Catnip tea quiets colic and can even be used to stop convulsions. It is also a sedative, and can soothe indigestion problems."

"I had no idea," I admitted as I turned the page in my notebook, and shook at my ink pen that was giving out on me. "Did you travel to other places?" I distractedly inquired as I felt through the bottom of my book bag, searching for another writing utensil.

"From there, I returned to the Monongahela Mountains for a few years and tinkered around with my newly discovered herbs, before planning a trip to the rainforest of Brazil."

"Brazil?" Allison chimed in, as her hand jerked the sink plug out and she slapped it down on the counter. "My dear departed husband took me to Brazil one time." She turned on the water to rinse out the sink. "Of course, I realize this is about Molly and her story, so I'll save my adventures for a later date." She busied herself with washing off the countertop.

"Brazil," Molly whispered as her face took on a dreamy state. "Another beautiful place to visit." She ran her hand unconsciously over her face, "I discovered the amazing qualities of Sangre de Grado, which erases wrinkles."

Allison's mouth gaped open, "You know the secret ingredient needed to acquire eternal youth?"

"No," Molly's nose crinkled in consternation, "I didn't say anything about eternal youth. I simply suggested the bright red plant resin helps with skin conditions. It boasts a rich array of flavonoids to rejuvenate skin cells and stimulate collagen production. This is how it effectively plumps and firms skin. It can also be used as an antibacterial, antifungal, and antiviral, so it helps cure bug bites, abrasions, cuts and even acne. You could add a drop on a pimple and it would be gone the next day."

I gazed at her as my eyes narrowed to tiny slits, "Molly, have you even noticed the pimples I have? I think you could have mentioned this earlier."

She reached over and tapped my hand, "Carolyn, you are a beautiful young woman. You don't need to change one single thing about yourself."

I was seriously considering taking Allison's side, concerning the debated refund issue surrounding the Bladderwrack order at this point, but managed to maintain my professionalism. "What else do you remember about the rainforest?"

"It is an amazing place for an herbal alchemist to live. It is the richest botanical resource in the world and contains around five million species of healing plants. I doubt it is known, even today, all the secret cures that can be found in the jungle. I would bet there is a cure for everything, just waiting to be discovered in the rainforest of Brazil."

"You are persistent," I complimented my friend.

Allison plopped down on a chair and scooted it up to the table, "She'll stick to it 'til the last pea is out of the pod."

We chuckled out loud, before a comfortable silence enveloped the kitchen.

As I stared out to the veranda and the trees beyond, I presumed this memoir was about wrapped up, then decided I better make sure there wasn't more to her tale, "Did you travel anywhere else in your pursuit of medicinal properties?" I asked half distractedly.

"Only one more," she admitted, "I spent several years in India learning about the Tree of Life, or what is called, Peepal.

"Peepal?" I repeated, "How do you spell that?"

"P-e-e-p-a-l" she enunciated.

"Thanks," I scratched through my rudimentary spelling, "what is it and how is it used?"

"The Tree of Life, or Peepal, is an amazing tree. Almost all parts of the tree such as bark, fruit, seeds, shoots and latex are used for medicinal and therapeutic purposes. Some of the compounds found in this amazing tree are steroids, tannins, and flavonoids. It is believed to cure diseases such as diarrhea, hemorrhoids, gonorrhea and inflammations. Its leaves serve as a wonderful laxative, and to get rid of mumps and boils. In addition, the roots of the plant are chewed to prevent gum diseases and the powered form of its fruit is taken for asthma. It has many wonderful qualities."

"It sounds like a miracle tree," I admitted.

"Some folks feel it is." Molly agreed. "God gave us many trees, flowers, spices and herbs to help us in this life, and I am privileged to have learned so much about the abundant bounty provided by our Lord."

I clicked my pen, and laid it on the table. "You have had an amazing life, Molly, this is for sure."

Allison, once more, pushed for her refund.

"Fine," Molly gave in, "hand me my purse and I'll give you three dollars."

"No," Allison shook her head, "it's too late now."

I giggled at the elderly women's banter. "Alrighty then, I'm going to write this up and I will get back with you in about a week to see if I missed anything. If you think of anything you would like to add, just jot down a note because we will be editing and checking the spelling of these plants." I bundled everything up and slid it into my backpack. "Thanks for sharing your stories with me, Molly. It has been a pleasure."

"I told you," Allison waggled her finger in my direction, "this woman has experienced a remarkable life."

As I rose from my chair, Allison hopped up too. "I have to scurry off," she said over her shoulder as she slid the stiff patio door open. "Molly, I'll be back in about an hour. Let's get spruced up in our Sunday best and have a nice dinner somewhere special," we could hear her shout, as she launched her leg over the railing of the patio.

Later the same evening, Molly heard someone banging on her front door as she was brushing her teeth, so she thought she had better answer, just in case there was a fire or some other emergency. She spit the toothpaste into the sink, then with toothbrush in hand, rushed to the front door. Molly peered through the peephole only to spy Allison's enormously magnified eye staring back at her. She slid the chain from the lock and opened the door wide, as she sauntered back into the bathroom. Allison followed behind at her heels.

"There is an eligible bachelor that wants to meet you this evening, Molly." Allison nodded ardently, as she scanned the spacious yellow-tiled bathroom.

Molly turned toward her and propped her hand on her hip, "I have no interest in meeting anyone, Allison."

"Interested or not, he is stopping by to meet you in less than an hour. You need to put on your knee-highs," she leaned in close to Molly's face, "and probably add a touch of lipstick."

"Allison, I told you before, I am not interested in meeting a man at my age. The only gleam in my eyes is when the sun hits my bifocals. I am perfectly content with my life," she shook her finger to emphasize the point, "just as it is."

"No. I'm serious." She insisted, "You're going to want to slide on your knee-highs and some shoes with a heel – your legs will look slimmer."

Molly peeked down at her bright red sundress, then to her flip-flops and back toward Allison, "No knee-highs!" She exasperatedly declared. "Why don't you just hook up with this eligible bachelor?"

"I'll admit he could leave his boots under my bed, anytime. However, this one is meant for you, I promise." She flashed a sideward grin, "Hurry up, he'll be here any minute." Allison started rummaging through the bag of cosmetics that was propped on the sink and victoriously plucked a tube of bright red lipstick out of the container. "Here you go, Molly. You need to brighten up your face."

Molly brushed her hand away, wondering if Allison had listened to a single word she had just conveyed. "No! I am serious. Absolutely, positively not!"

A disappointed look covered Allison's face as she stared at her friend incredulously. "Would you at least run a brush through your hair? Please? For me?"

Molly snatched the brush from her hand and quickly ran it through her thick gray curls. "Better?" she asked sarcastically. Allison discriminately looked Molly over and mumbled something not quite distinguishable, but Molly thought it had to do with knee-high hose.

They both froze when they heard a knock on the door.

"He's here," Allison was absolutely giddy.

Molly moaned theatrically as she followed her into the living room.

Allison took a look over her shoulder, "Are you ready?" She was practically jumping up and down with excitement akin to a toddler's.

Molly reasoned this visit could only last an hour. Tops. "Sure."

She opened the door and provided a welcoming gesture for the eligible bachelor to enter.

Honestly, Molly's jaw just about hit the floor when she saw an extremely good looking man, about her age, standing straight and tall with a smile that caused the folds in his cheeks to deepen as his mouth curved up at the corners. His eyes looked vaguely familiar. *"Is that a dimple in one of his cheeks?"*

Allison immediately provided introduction, "Molly, I am sure you remember Zach Moore." She offered a quick wink, "From the mountains of West Virginia?"

Molly immediately regretted not pulling on her knee-high hose.

"Molly?" Mr. Zach Moore whispered, "Do you remember me? From down at the witness tree? I went down there everyday until the family moved away, at the prospect of seeing you again." His heartfelt smile touched her deeply, "But you never showed up."

Molly felt a twinge of guilt stirring in her heart.

Zach didn't wait for a response, "You sure are a sight for

sore eyes, Molly Minion."

Molly gulped back a lump that had formed in her throat and forced back the fresh tears that had began to mist her eyes. "Of course, I remember you, Zach."

His arms stretched out to pull her close in a tight bear hug as, Woody, the cat brushed against his legs.

Allison stood with her hands grasped in front of her, grinnin' like the cat that got the canary, "Well, I'll just leave you two to catch-up. I'm going to meet Mr. Farmer for a walk."

"Mr. Farmer?" Molly restrained her comment, *"The pelvic thrusting pervert from the second floor?"* Molly forced the disturbing thought from her mind. "Just a minute, Allison." Molly peered questioningly over her shoulder, "How did you... how did you find Zach?"

"I told you," Allison shook her head agitatedly, "I could find a needle in a haystack, just like my husband. Didn't I tell you he was a private detective?" She thoughtfully ruminated for a brief second, "Yeah, I'm sure I did."

Zach and Molly stood staring into one another eyes, as the front door slapped shut behind Allison.

"What do ya say, Molly? Let's go outside and watch the clouds drift by?"

"That sounds like a wonderful idea, but I do need to warn you, there aren't any flying squirrels around these parts."

An intense chuckle seeped from his throat as his hand clutched Molly's hand, and together they strolled, in silence, outside to the petite veranda.

"Please have a seat," she motioned toward the chair.

"Thank you." He pulled the wrought iron chair closer to her. "I do believe I still owe you a trip to Seneca Rocks,"

Zack warmly suggested.

Molly beamed as she remembered their conversation from years ago, "I think I will take you up on that offer."

"Tell me, Molly Minion, what have you been up to these last seventy-four years?"

"Oh," she provided a casual flick of her hand, "nothing remarkable."

He tenderly glanced toward her before asking, "Did ya have a good life?"

Molly considered this question intently before replying. "Oh yes," she nodded enthusiastically as she leaned over and quietly confided, "out of all the people in this big ole world," she devoted a grateful wave of her hand to the skies, "God blessed me."

Her eyes sparkled heartily, "Can you believe it, Zach?" A reminiscent smile slowly wrapped up around her cheeks, "God blessed me!"

Molly refused to disclose specifics concerning her and Zach's trip to Seneca Rocks. She simply indicated her lips were sealed, as she ran her finger in a zipping motion across her mouth.

"Did you beg and plead for the fine points?" you ask.

Of course, I implored for hours, hoping desperately to share the particulars with you. I even asked if she had slipped Ginseng into his tea, but she puffed up and bluntly responded, "There was no need."

Regrettably, my attempt at collecting the assorted details needed to complete the conclusion of this portion of her memoir was unsuccessful, and after all, it isn't my secret to tell.

So, all I can assure is this... another chapter in Molly Minion's most remarkable life has blossomed, just like the wildflowers that push through the dense brown leaves carpeting the earth do every spring, in the gloriously wonderful mountains of West Virginia.

Best Regards,
Carolyn

"The remarkable thing is that it is the crowded life that is most easily remembered. A life full of turns, achievements, disappointments, surprises, and crises is a life full of landmarks. The empty life has even its few details blurred, and cannot be remembered with certainty." – Eric Hoffer

Author's Notes

Flying Squirrels – Zach and Molly enjoyed watching for the West Virginia northern flying squirrels. The squirrels live in high-elevation, spruce-northern hardwood forests of the Allegheny Highlands consisting of red spruce, fir, beech, yellow birch, sugar or red maple, hemlock and black cherry. The squirrel historically lived in the old-growth spruce forests that dominated the highlands until extensive industrial logging decimated this habitat between the 1880s and the 1940s. Even in the wake of this landscape level of habitat loss, West Virginia northern flying squirrels were resilient enough for a few residual populations to survive in small, scattered patches of less than ideal habitat while forests regenerated over the following decades.

With built-in parachutes, in the form of wing-like flaps of skin stretching from leg to leg, West Virginia northern flying squirrels glide among the trees in the mountains of Appalachia. Flying squirrels are the oldest living line of modern squirrels on the planet, having first appeared 30 million years ago. At home in the forest canopy and on the ground, these dexterous, and social critters have become a signature species of the West Virginia highlands.
http://www.fws.gov/northeast/newsroom/wvnfsq.html

Witness Trees - For years, surveyors marked the location of a survey corner using witness trees. Such was the case for the witness tree that marked the land adjoining the Minions' property to the Moores' property in this memoir. The trees were located near the survey corner and were inscribed with survey data. In land surveying, a property corner sometimes cannot be marked because the true point lies on a cliff or in a swamp, stream or lakebed. A witness tree is a large tree, so situated that it can serve as the reference point. Using old deeds and witness trees, a United States Forest Service scientist recently created a glimpse of the composition of the forests that covered today's Monongahela National Forest before settlement and logging changed the landscape.

http://www.sciencedaily.com/releases/2012/09/120912085040.htm

The Monongahela National Forest, where Molly grew up, is the only national forest that is completely within the boundaries of West Virginia. The Monongahela Forest includes some major landform features such as Spruce Knob, Seneca Rocks, and the western portion of the Ridge-and-Valley Appalachians. The first land was purchased in 1915, and on April 28, 1920, it became the Monongahela National Forest by presidential proclamation. In the late 19th and early 20th century, logging and timber operations had removed much of the hardwood stands of the Allegheny Mountains, causing serious ecological damage to these mountains and erosion along the streams. In March 1907, flooding devastated the land along the banks of the Monongahela River. As a result of this damage and damage to woodlands and streams in other areas of the United States, Congress enacted the Weeks Law in 1911, which authorized the federal government to cooperate with the various states to purchase land for the protection of the watersheds of navigable streams. Through other federal legislation, the purposes of the national forests were extended to include reforestation and timber production, wildlife management, and outdoor recreation. https://www.nationalforests.org/our-forests/find-a-forest/monongahela-national-forest

Seneca Rocks is a formation of sheer towering whitish rocks located near the confluence of Seneca Creek and the North Fork of the South Branch of the Potomac. In the early morning mist the jagged outline of Seneca Rocks resembles the bony back of a giant dinosaur. This vast mountain of pale stone whose rocks rise 1,000 feet from the forest floor and provides cliffs and lofty crags inviting exploration by birds, rock climbers, and agile visitors. The name comes from the Seneca Indians, who once used this vast wilderness for hunting, fishing, and trade routes. Today the Seneca Rocks area is part of the Monongahela National Forest.

http://www.wvencyclopedia.org/articles/241

The Flood of 1907, when Nina saved Molly from the raging rapids, took place when all rivers flowing southward into the Ohio River reached flood stage in March of 1907. Despite navigation dams, the lower Monongahela River also flooded heavily at this time, causing more than one hundred million dollars worth of damage along the river and in the city of Pittsburgh, Pennsylvania. Dozens of homes in Athens, Ohio were swept away, overturned, or lifted off their foundations by the raging Hocking River. Six hundred people were forced from their homes in Zanesville, Ohio. The flood inundated Portsmouth but with

temperatures reaching 70 degrees on Sunday, March 17th, thousands took advantage of the fine weather to row about the city's streets. The flood caused many deaths in the cities and towns throughout the region.
http://ohsweb.ohiohistory.org/swio/pages/content/1907_floods.htm

Following the 1964 Civil Rights Act, the West Virginia Legislature passed state laws, which fully enfranchise all citizens. It was again legal for Native Americans to own land in West Virginia and to indicate Native American ancestry on birth records. Nina was not alive to witness this notable triumph.
http://www.wvculture.org/arts/ethnic/native.html

The Weeks Act - March 1, 2011, marked the centennial of the Weeks Act, also known as the "organic act" of the eastern national forests. Signed into law by President William Howard Taft, the Weeks Act permitted the federal government to purchase private land in order to protect the headwaters of rivers and watersheds in the eastern United States and called for fire protection efforts through federal, state, and private cooperation. Although Pop and Nina did not choose to participate in this program, it has been one of the most successful pieces of conservation legislation in United States history. To date, the Weeks Act has protected nearly twenty million acres of forestland. This land provides habitat for hundreds of plants and animals, recreation space for millions of visitors, and economic opportunities for countless local communities. As one historian has noted, "No single law has been more important in the return of the forests to the eastern United

States."
http://www.foresthistory.org/ASPNET/Policy/WeeksAct/index.aspx

Joe Brown was a notorious character. He had earned the reputation of an outlaw for his crime of shooting Scott White, Chief of Police of Whitmer, and a son of Wash White, mayor of the same town. Waiting until the dead of night, when the streets of the town were deserted, between fifty and one hundred masked men, without creating a commotion, or disturbing the slumbers of the town, surrounded the jail, forced the two guards, at the point of revolvers, to vacate their posts and entered the jail. Brown was hustled from its protecting walls for a distance of about half a square, a noose adjusted around his neck, and hanged by block and tackle to a flagpole from which his inanimate body still dangled the next morning when the town awoke. After making sure that life was extinct, those involved in the lynching quietly dispersed.
http://www.wvculture.org/history/crime/lynchingbrown.html

Herbal Alchemy involves fermentation, distillation, and extraction of plant compounds, using organic, all-natural ingredients. The goal is to discover and create herbal medications and elixirs to help in the healing process. In the last decade, major medical centers have identified how selected herbs and spices can complement the prevention and management of chronic disorders.

Pop's favorite hymn was "His Eye is on the Sparrow" which was written in 1905, by Civillia D. Martin (lyricist), and

Charles H. Gabriel (composer).

Nina's Picture is licensed under Public Domain via Commons: "Ah-Weh-Eyu" by J.L. Blessing, published by The Blessing Studio, Salamanca, New York, United States - [1].
https://commons.wikimedia.org/wiki/File:Ah-Weh-Eyu.jpg
Seneca woman Ah-Weh-Eyu (Pretty Flower), 1908.

Nina's Herbal Remedies

Belladonna – used to treat whooping cough, and as a pain reliever.

Blackwort – used as an anti-inflammatory, and to heal cuts, bruises and sprains.

Bladderwrack – used to treat arthritis.

Butterbar – used to treat headaches.

Dandelions – used to treat upset stomach, joint and muscle pain.

Ginseng – used to treat forms of diabetes, as a stimulant, an aphrodisiac, and for male dysfunction.

Goatsfoot – used to treat gout.

Horsetail – used to treat kidney and bladder stones, as a weight loss supplement, for hair loss, and to ease the pain of frostbite.

Lady Smock – used to strengthen the heart.

Lavender – used to treat acne, headaches, and for circulation disorders.

Monkshood Root – used to treat fevers, skin diseases, joint and leg pain.

Note: Monkshood is a very toxic herb, which should be used with extreme caution.

Sage – used to strengthen the nervous system, improve memory, and sharpen the senses.

White Bryony – used to treat infected wounds, and as a laxative.

"Thank ya for reading Molly's Memoir"

Printed in the USA
CPSIA information can be obtained
at www.ICGtesting.com
LVHW040031091023
760539LV00006B/393